IMAGES
of America

LIVE OAK COUNTY

An oxcart road ran through what would become Live Oak County. North of Laredo, it veered right from Laredo-Bexar Road before entering Live Oak County (its outline superimposed on this 1833 map). The road crossed the Nueces River north of present-day George West. Oxcart wheels squeaked loudly through vast thickets of cacti. The same plant that fed the Indians greased oxcart wheels. (Author's collection.)

ON THE COVER: Tom Nance sits behind the wheel with a passenger who has just detrained to purchase land. Nance worked cattle when not operating a taxi service. George West rode the train from San Antonio in his personal Pullman to meet with Will Blackmon, a former Texas Ranger hired to build West's namesake town. With the arrival of the railroad, Three Rivers and George West grew. Bypassed towns, however, withered and died. (Courtesy Patrick Burns.)

IMAGES
of America

LIVE OAK COUNTY

Richard Hudson and Janis Hudson

ARCADIA
PUBLISHING

Published by Arcadia Publishing
Charleston, South Carolina

Library of Congress Control Number: 2011943057

For all general information, please contact Arcadia Publishing:
Telephone 843-853-2070
Fax 843-853-0044
E-mail sales@arcadiapublishing.com
For customer service and orders:
Toll-Free 1-888-313-2665

Visit us on the Internet at www.arcadiapublishing.com

Dedicated to Live Oak pioneers and descendants, especially Mary Jane "Janie" (Brister) Hudson, whose forbearers were among the first to brave this timeless frontier.

CONTENTS

ACKNOWLEDGMENTS

We are forever grateful to James and Liz Stewart for their hospitality, encouragement, inspiration, and support while we researched and composed this book. It made our work easier. We began to list the other Live Oak County people who helped in this project, but found their numbers too great for the space allowed. We thank all who opened their doors and shared family photographs and stories, all done with warm Texas hospitality.

Some individuals call for special recognition. As chairman for the Armantrout Museum, Jim Warren welcomed us to a valuable resource, accompanying us on many excursions into the brush. Roger Stewart, son of photographer Stanley Stewart, opened an immense storehouse of his father's photographs, as did Patrick Burns for the West story, and Eugenia Thorn for the Charles Tips family. The hospitality and historical resources of Kurt House were a valuable contribution. We must also mention Buddy Jones, Roberta Dobie, Patty Reagan, Mary Margaret Campbell, and John and Sue Holland, who shared caches of collected photographs and information from many sources. Their help was invaluable.

Live Oak County's wealth of writers and resources yielded local and outside documentation, listed in the bibliography. We extend many thanks to those who shared titles previously unknown to us.

Organizations and sites that demonstrated superior civic services were the libraries of George West and Three Rivers; Dolph Briscoe Center for American History, Austin; Michener Center for Writers, Austin; South Texas Museum, Alice; Southwest Texas Community College, Uvalde; Buckhorn Saloon and Museum, San Antonio; Texas Highway Department, Austin; Texas State Archives, Austin; *Beeville Picayune*, Beeville; and *Corpus Christi Caller*, Corpus Christi.

Our excellent Arcadia editors, Lauren Hummer and Laura Bruns, patiently guided us to the finish line. Thank you so much.

To contact the authors for additional information, please visit www.historyraven.com.

INTRODUCTION

Multiple considerations became evident while researching, compiling photographs, and writing the history of Live Oak County. The richness of its past and current pioneers is vast. The scope of this publication limits the depth of each topic. Because of this, we endeavored to include representative people, places, and events that communicate the human and environmental spirit of this land. These choices required painful cuts. For every picture chosen, others were withheld for future publication. Space limitations of the book, those who consider their family history unimportant, the loss of records and photographs in devastating floods, and the number of former Live Oak residents who live elsewhere, all contribute to the acute brevity of what can be covered here. No bias was intended; we recognize that each story needs to be shared for future posterity. Therefore, this is a beginning. As we continue our research into the history of Live Oak County, we encourage readers to contact us via our website (www.historyraven.com) and continue with us on this path of revelation.

Live Oak County is a timeless frontier. The people who live here have inherited the indomitable spirit of their pioneering ancestors. In the known beginning, this land was covered with prairie grass. As natural shifts in climate occurred, wet and dry seasons alternated, riverbeds gave birth to pecan and live oak, great expanses of land developed mottes, and wildlife found refuge. Dry areas transformed into immense prickly pear fields. Acacia, huisache, hackberry, and mesquite crept in, transforming open grasslands into brush country.

Mastodons once shared this land with smaller wildlife. Centuries passed, and primordial beasts gave way to large panthers, wildcats, and coyotes. These animals preyed on javelina, bobcats, deer, rabbits, smaller mammals, and reptiles.

Into this land of beauty and harshness came early man, following riverbeds and fishing and living off roots, nuts, cacti tunas, reptiles, rodents, and small mammals. Humans carved out a meager subsistence. Travelers from the coastal plains and far western mountains interacted with the area's indigenous peoples. Slowly, over centuries, better tools were developed for snaring and killing wildlife for food, shelter, and clothing. Even though communication was primal, these hunter-gatherer groups used a similar language, now called Coahuiltecan. Then came men from other worlds, and life began rapidly changing.

Cabeza de Vaca may have been the first white man to travel through this land. Depicting the primitive life of its inhabitants, he was definitely the first to record its diverse and challenging ecology. De Vaca and his companions were lost; but once they found their *compadres* in Mexico, the stories they wrote sparked large campaigns of soldiers seeking fortune and monks seeking souls. The natives, over several more centuries and through intermarriage and work, assimilated the language and customs of the Spanish, becoming cohabitants with them.

The Spanish claimed this land far into the north, but Live Oak primarily served as a passageway to better and richer lands. Emerging from Mexico through what is now Live Oak County, oxcart roads wound their way into the tall pinewoods of East Texas and on to Louisiana. These East Texas paths often followed prehistoric roads built by Caddo and eventually embellished by Cherokee Indians, who planted bushes of tiny, pale-pink roses, which remain along the highways today. Other roads proceeded from Mexico north to San Antonio and crossed rivers and shallow creeks where natural rock beds existed. Later, ferries conveyed wagons and produce across the Nueces as more roads stretched up from Mexico. These roads converged at Puente de la Piedra, a natural bartering spot on Sulphur Creek. The site eventually became known as "On the Sulphur." By 1856, the fledgling town of Oakville came into being.

In the meantime, Karankawa, Lipan, and Comanche tribes became increasingly hostile as they experienced pressure from encroaching Spanish. French and Anglo Americans intruded from the Northeast. Indian aggression pressured not only the less aggressive Coahuiltecans, but also the Spaniards. The Spanish offered large grants of land in their northern territory to protect interior Mexico from Indian depredations, including the threat from American and French expansion. While successful rancheros and villas developed along the delta of the Rio Grande, only a few Spanish land grants were settled along rivers in the tougher brushlands, none to the east of the Nueces. The Ramirez brothers finally built a large rock-fortified hacienda called Fort Ramirez overlooking Ramireña Creek west of the Nueces River. Before their Spanish grant could be settled, they and most of their company were killed and routed by Indian attack. After Mexico won its independence from Spain in 1824, the Mexican government partially paid the Ramirez descendants for their loss. Time, weather, and treasure hunters removed most of the fort, except for a few large rocks now almost swallowed by the ground and brush.

Failure to settle Spaniards or Mexicans in the northern Mexican states of Texas, Santander, and Coahuila prompted Spain, and then Mexico, to approve Irish immigration. Among this new wave were James McGloin and John McMullen, who were granted land known as the San Patricio Colony and authorized to settle 200 Catholic families from their homeland. This proved a challenge, but those who came were hardy, brave, and steadfast. Some moved farther north along the Nueces River, using it for transportation. Ferry crossings made it easier for close colonization. Texas won its independence from Mexico in 1836 and joined the United States as the 28th state in 1845.

McGloin, Pugh, O'Docharty, Fox, Nation, James, Dougherty, and Lewis were but a few of the Irish names settling in what became Gussetville and Lagarto. Others settled on higher ground near the Sulphur around Oakville. Indian, Mexican, and Anglo American outlaws made trips to San Patricio dangerous. Men of the area met under a spreading live oak tree between Gussetville and Oakville in 1856 to sign a petition for a separate county. After the state ratified Live Oak County, Oakville, near the old oxcart crossing on Sulphur Creek, was chosen as the county seat. During the Civil War, a mixed breed of Mexican and American cattle called Longhorns grew approximately seven million strong. After the war, the romance of the West began as cowboys on horseback herded these cattle north to feed a war-weary nation.

By the turn of the 20th century, railroads connected most of the country, and ways of life changed rapidly. Cattle drives to market gave way to rail transportation. Towns died and new ones began. Live Oak County was no less affected by the railroad. Three Rivers and George West sprang up to become centers of activity and commerce. Other towns, bypassed by railroads, languished and died.

During the past 100 years, Live Oak County has transitioned, along with the nation, into new ways of living and working. Oil, gas, and uranium changed the county's economic base in the 1920s. Today, new technologies bring new challenges and new frontiers. We hope readers find unexpected and surprising delights in this visual reflection of Live Oak County's timeless frontier.

One

DAWNING

A COUNTY RISES FROM A PRIMORDIAL PAST

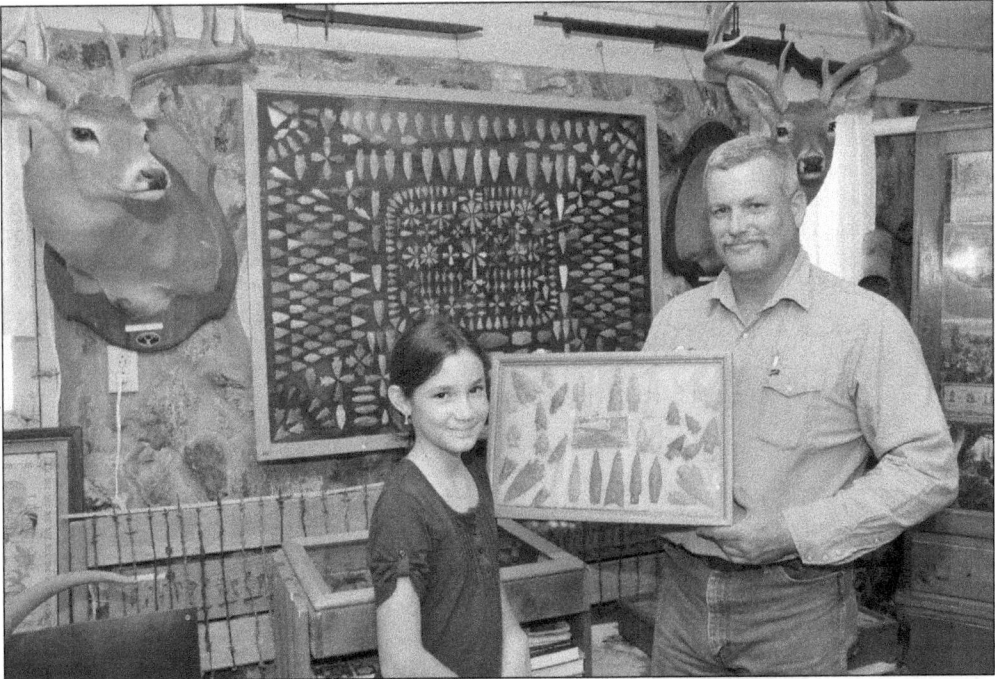

Professional archeologists and laymen find relics and specimens of a timeless frontier preserved in the caliche hills, sandstone, and valleys of Live Oak County. Here, Kip Dove and his daughter, Sadie, display arrowheads and early tools found by Kip's father, Homer, and grandfather, William Edward "Bud," as they worked the Las Palomas Ranch, which is now 100 years old. (Author's collection.)

In the 1970s, Loma Sandia, an archaeological dig just three miles from Three Rivers, produced a massive burial ground of more than 200 graves dating between 825 BC and about 1200 AD. The Universities of Texas at Austin and San Antonio, Texas A&M University, Texas Tech, and the highway department formed the largest archaeological-historical study in South Texas. Along the Frio River and its tributaries, two burial levels separated by centuries span archaic to prehistoric time. Bronzed aborigines roamed riverbeds while summer cacti, autumn nuts, and small game sustained them. Following creek beds in autonomous family groups with similar dialect, these ancient people left a small imprint and changed little, even into the sixteenth century when Cabeza de Vaca penned his record. Loma Sandia significantly changed the way archaeologists and historians view these ancient people. (Courtesy Center for Archaeological Research, Accession #CAR525, The University of Texas at San Antonio.)

Through Spanish Texas, Mexican oxcarts moved freight across dirt roads from Laredo to Goliad and Louisiana. Later, another road ran from Brownsville to San Antonio. Where the roads crossed near Sulphur Creek in future Live Oak County, travelers exchanged information and bartered commodities. Some built crude shelters and settled. (Courtesy Mary Margaret Campbell.)

The town of Barlow's Ferry, named for the crossing on the Nueces River, was later named Dinero (Spanish for "money") because of legends of buried treasure. Miller's Ferry, near Lagarto, provided passage via the Nueces to Matamoros in Mexico. Reportedly, members of Santa Anna's army marched to the Alamo and retreated from San Jacinto using the bedrock crossing at Sulphur Creek (Puente de la Piedra) near Oakville. (Courtesy Mary Margaret Campbell.)

The McMullen-McGloin Colony stretched northwest from San Patricio. The Nueces River comprised its southern boundary. After Texas independence, San Patricio became the county seat. Because of depredations by Indian, Mexican, and Anglo American desperadoes, the journey from the interior to the county seat was dangerous. Leaders, meeting near Gussettville, beneath the live oak tree shown above, wrote a petition to the state legislature to create a new county, named Live Oak. It became official on February 2, 1856. Below, descendants of those who signed the charter gathered to honor the original petitioners and place a state historical marker beneath the massive tree. Shown here are, from left to right: (standing in front) Robert William Strause; (first row) Patrick James, Pat Dougherty, Charles Wilson Campbell, Byron Hinton, and William Toudouze Jr.; (second row) Richard Ray Pugh and Willie Pugh James. (Author's collection and Bryan Hinton.)

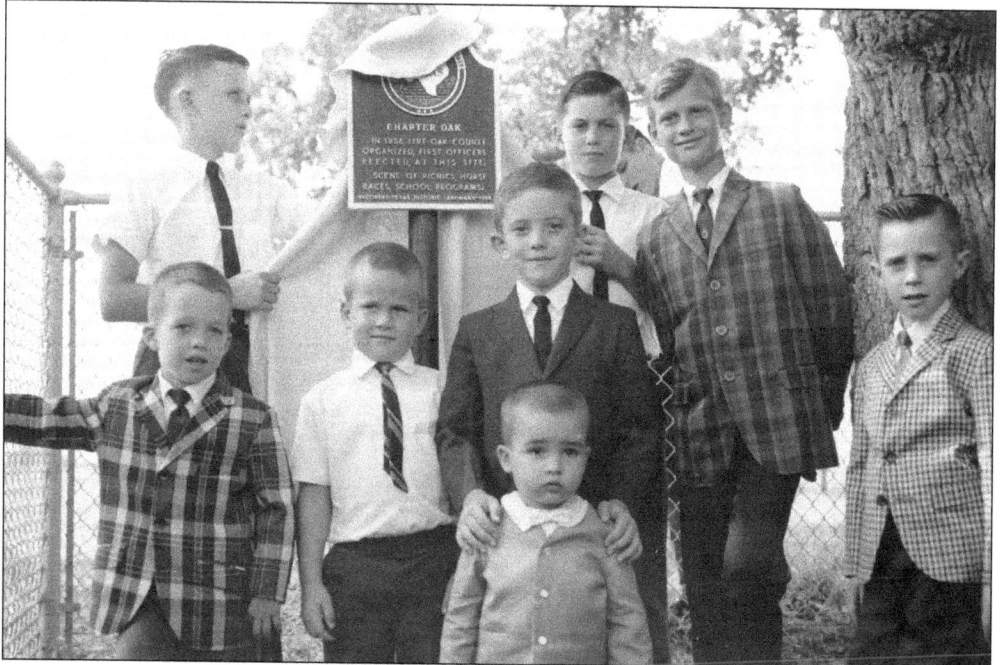

Two

STAGE STOPS AND SETTLEMENTS

BEFORE THE RAILROAD CHANGED LIVE OAK

Brush Arbor School - 1884
Lagarto, Live Oak County, Texas
Western Histories Collection, U. of Oklahoma

Early pioneers were people of education. Among them were teachers, musicians, engineers, lawyers, and doctors who wanted their children educated. Soon, communities built crude one-room, clapboard schoolhouses. Eventually, as resources permitted, brick buildings were erected. Brush arbors, such as this one in Lagarto about 1884, offered students and teacher cool respite from late spring and early autumn heat. (Courtesy Oklahoma University Southwest Collection.)

Live Oak was a passageway from the Rio Grande northeast to Goliad and Louisiana. At left, Jim Jackson (left) and Jim Warren stand beside a monument marking the ranch founded by the Ramirez brothers, who built a rock house/fortification about 1800 overlooking Ramireña Creek. When Spanish troops left South Texas in 1813, Lipan Indians attacked the Ramirez ranch, killing those unable to escape. Descendants later received compensation from the Mexican government for their loss. That was the first and last known ranch in the area until the Irish settled the McGloin-McMullen Grant in 1829. Later, a stagecoach stop and a post office and store were built at Ramireña. The old fort was on Dobie land. J. Frank Dobie records how weather and treasure-seekers destroyed the ruins. He is standing at right in the below photograph. Posing with him is most likely Prisciliano Chapa. (Left, author's collection; below, courtesy Michener Center for Writing.)

14

Patrick McGloin, Empresario McGloin's nephew, received a grant in 1831 on which the Fox and Nation families from San Patricio settled. Named Fox Nation, the area had a stagecoach stop and the area's first Catholic church. Norwich Gusset (right) opened a store in 1850, and the people renamed the community Gussetville. After losing the county seat, Gusset sold to S.W. Lewis and bought Gov. E.J. Davis's home on Broadway in Corpus Christi. Gusset established a successful merchant fleet from Corpus Christi to New York. Gussetville began to fade after losing the railroad. St. Joseph's Catholic Church remains, including a well-kept historical cemetery on Guy James's property, where, in the below photograph, Lamar James stands among family headstones. The cemetery holds the history of the Irish pioneers whom Margaret (Goynes) Olson immortalized in *Texas Roots*. (Right, courtesy Mary Margaret Campbell; below, author's collection.)

15

James McGloin's daughter, Elizabeth, and her husband, Patrick J. Murphy, built a store at Echo (pronounced "eeko"), overlooking the Nueces River. Elizabeth's sister, Margaret Mary (Healey), with her husband, John Bernard Murphy (left), bought part of the land in 1850. By 1855, the couple had moved to the two-story home (below) that still stands today, though it has been renovated from the original Victorian. Patrick and Elizabeth operated a grocery/dry-goods store, a stagecoach stop, and an inn for passengers. The stagecoach stop was used by Jim Drury as he rode horseback to deliver mail from saddlebags between Corpus Christi and San Antonio. Shortly before the Civil War, John Bernard and Margaret Mary Murphy moved to Corpus Christi, where John practiced law and became the mayor. He died in 1884 after a brief illness. (Left, courtesy Andi Estes; below, author's collection.)

After John Murphy's death, Margaret Mary bought the stagecoach inn and returned to Echo. Visiting San Antonio, she was appalled to see homeless children of emancipated slaves roaming the streets. She dedicated her life and income to helping these children. Within two years, she became a consecrated nun and founded St. Peter Claver Academy, a school and home still in operation today. The below photograph shows a 1950s graduation at the academy. For 10 years, Margaret Mary brought nuns to Echo from Ireland, including her sister, who studied Spanish and received training for teaching in the academy. Margaret Mary founded the order called the Sisters of the Holy Spirit and Mary the Immaculate and established a San Antonio convent in 1892 named Our Lady of Light. (Right, courtesy Andi Estes; below, courtesy the Sisters of the Holy Spirit.)

Lagarto College, a liberal arts school, operated from 1884 to 1895. Its staff included President Dr. A.G. Heaney from New York, Superintendent W.Y. Taylor, and about eight teachers for both lower grades and higher education. Ella Jane Byer, later J. Frank Dobie's mother, was among the noted teachers. Samuel Francis Beall, a gifted violin student, received a Stradivarius from his teacher for exceptional achievement. (Courtesy Mary Beth Hinnant.)

Edna (Adams) Beall and her daughters Lena (center) and Ruth ride in a carriage. The Beall family, originally from Scotland, owned and operated a general merchandise store during Lagarto's best years. Ranchers around Lagarto vacillated about giving right-of-way to the Aransas Pass San Antonio Railroad. In the end, the railroad missed Lagarto by 11 miles, leading to Lagarto's demise. The Bealls' store was the last to close. (Courtesy Jessica Keese.)

Deputy Marshal Charles Henry Vanvalkenburg "Charley" Fusselman (second row, center) joined Texas Ranger Company D. Sergeant Fusselman, while pursuing rustlers in the Franklin Mountains near El Paso, was killed by Geronimo Parra. Sheriff Pat Garrett delivered Parra for trial and hanging. The canyon where the shooting occurred is known as Fusselman Canyon. Fusselman is buried with family in Lagarto Cemetery. (Courtesy Buckhorn Saloon and Museum.)

Lagarto ("alligator" in Spanish) was already a bustling community when John W. Ramey laid out its streets in 1856. The first store, built by James Rather, was sold in 1875 to Henry B. Newberry. In this photograph, Sarah Frances (Boatwright) Newberry stands on the porch next to Henry. Their son, Jim Henry, worked for the railroad and married Elizabeth Ellen Beall. (Courtesy Jessica Keese.)

Fort Merrill was established on a hill overlooking a bend of the Nueces River in southeast Live Oak County on March 1, 1850, by Capt. Samuel M. Plummer and Companies H and K of the 1st US Infantry. Their job: protect settlers, travelers on the road between Corpus Christi and San Antonio, and supply wagons from Army headquarters in Corpus Christi to frontier forts. Archeologist and historian Jim Warren, using authentic documents, described the daily operations and lives of the troops in *The Fort Merrill Letters*, available from the Armantrout Museum in George West. The fort was abandoned on December 1, 1855, and Confederate soldiers used it during the Civil War. The buildings are gone now. A gray granite monument placed in 1936 on private ranch property marks the site. An old cemetery sits up the hill under a motte of massive live oaks. It is said the fort was named in honor of Capt. Moses E. Merrill, killed during the Mexican-American War in the battle of Molino del Rey on September 8, 1847. (Author's collection.)

Zella (McCampbell) Weston, a freed slave of Judge Jim Anderson McCampbell, married Tom Weston, a free man from Mier, Mexico. They inherited 2,000 acres from the judge on which they built a small community called Anna Rose. Their marriage was accepted even though it was unlawful at the time. Tom and Zella's daughter, Pinkie, and her husband, Romano Chapa, lived on 600 inherited acres. Pinkie and Romano owned a popular dance hall at Anna Rose. Pinkie's brothers, Atlee and Nob, were respected cowboys. In the above photograph, family members Memrie Waters (left), Robert Mark Montes (center), and Mackey Alvarez attend a Weston reunion in 2000. Below, Otila Martinez reads the writing on the back of a photograph of her mother, Pinkie. (Courtesy *Corpus Christi Caller.*)

Alexander Coker, 18 at the time, enlisted in Company H, Texas 11th Cavalry on July 20, 1861. He fought in the Battle of Stones River, which had the highest percentage of casualties on both sides of any battle during the Civil War. Miraculously, Coker survived uninjured. Granted special leave in the summer of 1864, Coker returned to Live Oak to restore law and order as county sheriff. He served two separate terms in that capacity and one term as county treasurer. (Courtesy Kurt House.)

John Sanderson Campbell, a Pennsylvania cabinetmaker, became a Union captain during the Civil War. Campbell moved to Live Oak County after the war and married Minnie Ophelia Bartlett. The Campbells had six children: Nathan Ransom, Minnie Lee (later Cunningham), Lucy (later Weathersby), Beulah Mae (later Webb), Pauline (Gray), and Charles Sanderson. Pres. William McKinley appointed Campbell postmaster for Oakville in 1901, and he served until 1908. (Courtesy Cody Campbell.)

J.C.C. Hill's indomitable spirit caused Mexico's General Ampudia to adopt him during the fatal Mier Expedition. Upon taking charge, Santa Anna released Hill from Ampudia's adoption and provided Hill with an education, including civil engineering. Hill repaid the kindness by surveying and supervising railroad construction throughout Mexico. W.A. Hill, J.C.C.'s nephew, became county judge of Live Oak in 1899 and mayor of Three Rivers in 1927. (Author's collection.)

The first county fair was held in Oakville in 1916. People came from all around to show off their prized animals, needlework, canned goods, agriculture products, and to just have a good visit. Among the people posing in this photograph are Felix Crawford, Tom Church, E.F. Hatfield, Woody Tullis, Andrew Tullis, a Mr. Ashley, Pete Lawley, John Sanderson Campbell, and W.J. McMurray. (Courtesy Buddy Jones.)

23

Simmons City children rarely saw snow. On this occasion, W.C. Matkin (right) and his children, Reagan (left), Hontice (second from left), and Bill make the most of a day off from school. Behind them is Matkin's Store, across from the Godwin Hotel. Simmons Community Church is behind the store, and the windmill on the right supplied fresh water for the community. (Courtesy Lois Matkin.)

Simmons, like all of Live Oak County, is known for hunting. Each season produces new trophies. During early settlement years, deer and turkey were common table fare. Wild panthers, cougars, bobcats, mountain lions, coyotes, javelinas, and other animals were a plentiful menace. Bounties were placed on them by the state, and meticulous records were kept as hunters brought specimens in for payment. (Courtesy Lois Matkin.)

Strenuous farm and ranch labor prepared young Live Oak men and women for World War II. William "Bill" Hudson (left) was one of 510 who joined the military after the December 7, 1941, attack on Pearl Harbor. Of those troops, 46 never returned home. Many, like brother and family man Fred Hudson, worked stateside to support the war effort. Fred became a community leader in Simmons. (Courtesy Dean Hudson-Morton.)

H.D. Jr. and Mildred (Clayton) House were active in Simmons. Mildred graduated from Simmons school, where H.D.'s father taught and later served as principal. The House family engaged in various enterprises, including drilling some of the first shallow oil wells around Simmons. In Three Rivers, H.D. Jr. and Mildred continued to play leading roles in community affairs. In later years, Mildred traveled extensively worldwide. (Courtesy Kurt House.)

The 1920 Simmons girls' basketball team played half-court basketball on a dirt court. Tennis was also played on dirt. These players' uniforms were homemade. In the first row, far left, is Gladys Farrier (Hudson) and on the far right is Thelma Hicks (Hudson). Other teammates identified alphabetically are: Corrinne Autry, Martha Carroll, Lillie Cleveland, and Nora Sawyer. One player is unidentified. (Courtesy Lois Matkin.)

Preparing a barbecue for Mildred Blaschke and Dudley Bellows' wedding at Ray Point are, from left to right, Coke Braune, unidentified, Henry Magel, and Edmund Braune. Barbecue has been a longtime Texas staple. In *Longhorns*, Dobie tells of rancher Cal Wright finding a meatless meal at Ed McWhorter's. Cal exclaimed, "anybody hungry can eat . . . beef, provided it's not wasted and the hide's saved. That's the way we all feel." (Courtesy Mildred Bellows.)

26

Three

THREE RIVERS

BORN ON THE FOURTH OF JULY, 1913

Annie Hamilton offered $5,000 to the San Antonio, Uvalde, & Gulf Railroad to come through her Live Oak County ranch. Charles Tips organized the Hamiltonburg Township, later changed to Three Rivers to avoid confusion with another Texas town, and paid the $5,000. A July 4, 1913, grand opening lot sale and barbeque drew homesteaders and entrepreneurs. Fred Harris's "jitney" (taxi) service drove customers over dirt streets cut from thorny brush and cacti to view the lots for sale. (Courtesy Stanley Stewart.)

Advertisements drew farmers and entrepreneurs of Anglo, Mexican, German, Irish, French, Polish, and Czech descent to Hamiltonburg. In the background of this photograph, horse races are taking place at the far eastern end of Thornton street. In the lower left, Charles Tips is expounding investment opportunities in Hamiltonburg from an open car. Directly in front of Tips stands Clint Lippard in gray Gatsby and coat. Newspaperman James Cunningham, who owned the first home and the first business in Hamiltonburg, stands on the sidewalk in black bowler and suit. (Courtesy Eugenia Thorn.)

Charles Tips and his future bride, Hazel Woodward, of San Antonio, pose early in 1913. At the age of 19 and newly graduated from the University of Texas, Tips envisioned becoming the last "empresario" in Texas by building a town at the confluence of the Atascosa, Frio, and Nueces Rivers to serve a vast farming and ranching community. (Courtesy Eugenia Thorn.)

Charles Tips was the first citizen of Three Rivers, and his assistant, Pat Swearingen, the second. The first structure was a tent, which served as a temporary real estate office and living quarters for both men. The tent was later replaced by House Hardware. Next, Tips built the Three Rivers Hotel across from the tent and moved his office and living quarters into it. Because Swearingen, whose father was a judge on the court of civil appeals in San Antonio, could speak fluent Spanish, he supervised land clearing and street construction. Clearing crews were paid $6 per acre, based on the price established by the railroad. A telephone line from Oakville to a telephone in Tips's tent made him the proud owner and operator of the town's first telephone system. Besides business, Tips frequently engaged in long and costly evening telephone conversations with his fiancée, Hazel Underwood, in San Antonio. Tent structures similar to Tips's office provided families temporary shelter while building their homes. (Courtesy Eugenia Thorn.)

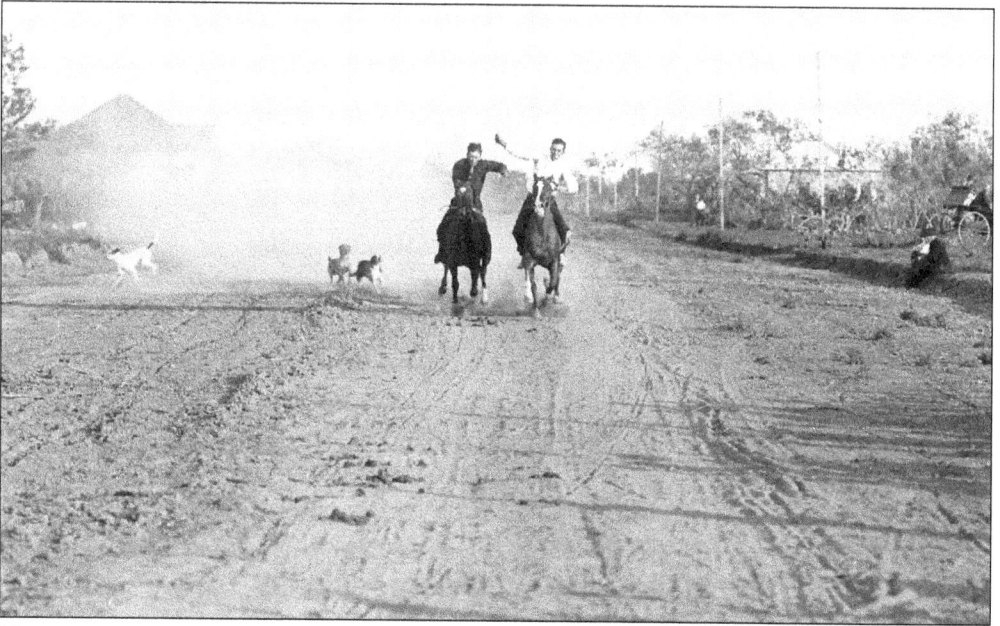

Horse racing and bronco busting provided entertainment at Tips's barbeque and lot sales extravaganzas. Horses and riders lined up in front of James Cunningham's house (roofline at upper left) at the far east end of Thornton Street, which offered the ideal dirt track. Raucous spectators urged their favorite picks onward to the finish string, held taut by Willie McMurray and James Cunningham. Winners received prizes. County ranches produced some of the fastest and best-trained cattle-working horses in Texas. (Courtesy Eugenia Thorn.)

Charles Tips's Hamiltonburg grand opening and lot sale held on July 4, 1913, drew thousands of celebrants and prospective buyers. Large, multicultural crowds were feted with barbeque, horse racing, and prizes. Conferring with Tips is Oakville rancher Henderson Coquat (standing at center left), who quit teaching to assist Tips. Coquat served as the town's first mayor and first school board chairman, and he drilled the first oil and gas wells in the county. (Courtesy Stanley Stewart.)

Tips contracted monstrous steam tractors from Corpus Christi to clear brush for the town and the surrounding fields. The machines were owned by a Mr. Bowles, seen sitting in the Model T Ford. This tractor pulled three moldboard plows to turn the soil. On the donkey, 10-year-old Cecil Cunningham sits ready to shoot scurrying rats and angry rattlesnakes driven from their habitat by the intruding tractor. (Courtesy Stanley Stewart.)

Mexican crews were contracted to clear land for streets and lots on which to build. Whole families camped near their work. While men grubbed cactus and brush, the women and children made huge piles to burn. The glow from these burning piles evoked a sense of tranquil bliss at night as Charles Tips sat watching from the wooden steps of his tent, beneath a starry sky. (Courtesy Stanley Stewart.)

James Cunningham moved the *Live Oak County Leader* building from Oakville to Hamiltonburg in 1913. First published in Oakville in June 1891, the paper was purchased by Cunningham, who began publication December 1, 1899, with "a Washington hand-press and a shirt-tail full of old-style, worn-out type." Harvey Evans (left) ran the press while Cunningham (right) gathered news. In 1925, the newspaper was renamed *Three Rivers News.* (Courtesy Stanley Stewart.)

James Cunningham's son, Cecil, worked at the newspaper in high school. His father died in 1948, yet Cecil continued delivering local news with the same dependable regularity as had his father. In the 1970s, the *News* merged with the *Live Oak County Herald* to become *The Progress of Live Oak and McMullen Counties*, which Collis Sellman bought in 1977. The newspaper's current owner, *Beeville Bee-Picayune*, staffs a Three Rivers news office. (Courtesy Margaret Custer.)

Oscar and Emil Voges moved the building in the above photograph from Boerne, in Kendall County, about 30 miles northwest of San Antonio, in 1913 to open a grocery called The Peoples' Cooperative Store. Standing in the doorway are, from left to right, Theresa Brownson, Adolph Stendebach, and Oscar Voges. Later, Clyde Owens opened a furniture store in the building, and in the 1930s, Herbert Symm had a beer tavern on the premises called The Green Inn. Symm's son continued the business after his father's death until April 1980, bringing their tenure to almost 50 years. Today, Rick Sowell's BBQ & Home Cooking occupies the building (below). The establishment serves up a tasty choice of Tex-Mex home cooking, bodacious barbeque, and chicken-fried steak. The building turns 100 years old in 2013. (Above, courtesy Stanley Stewart; below, author's collection.)

Charles Tips (at the steering wheel in the car) built the Three Rivers Hotel in 1913 for Fred Lippard, who employed the DeHavers (standing with dog next to the car) to manage the hotel. A grand ball was held in the hotel during the First Annual Live Oak County Land Show, held on November 15, 1913. The event drew 5,000 potential land buyers. Later owners of the hotel were the Monyhans, Mrs. Eitts, and Ma Hutchins. (Courtesy Stanley Stewart.)

The first hardware store in town was built by W.E. "Ed" McMurray. His ancestors emigrated from Ireland to the McGloin-McMullen Colony in the late 1830s, when Texas was a republic. Ed and his wife were among the first Oakville residents to move to Three Rivers. In the late 1920s, their unmarried daughter, Morine, taught in the Three Rivers Mexican School. Ed also served Three Rivers as justice of the peace. (Courtesy Stanley Stewart.)

Majors Drug Store was the first pharmacy in the new town. Standing in the doorway, E.G. Majors (left), Mrs. Majors (center), and Thressa Bronson are ready to help customers with such drugs as sulfur, which, mixed with molasses, was a treatment for rheumatism and purifying blood; alum and vinegar, to address sore throats; and various other tonics for invigorating, restoring, refreshing, stimulating, and healing the body. (Courtesy Stanley Stewart.)

In 1915, Charles Tips built a two-story house (currently being restored) on Thornton Street for his bride, San Antonio socialite Hazel Woodward. During construction, they lived in a room at the Three Rivers Hotel. While Tips managed the glass factory, a second, larger two-story house was purchased in 1928 on Murray Hill. This home served the Tips family for 10 years. After it burned down, the family returned to San Antonio. (Courtesy Eugenia Thorn.)

Contractor George Smith built the first house in Three Rivers, on Thornton Street, for newspaperman James Cunningham. The Cunninghams cooked their meals over a campfire while both their home and the newspaper office were being completed. Their children attended the first Three Rivers one-room, yellow schoolhouse, which had a single teacher for grades one through seven. Five generations of Cunninghams attended Three Rivers schools. (Courtesy Stanley Stewart.)

The Slabinsky family moved into Charles Tips's farmhouse and cared for his 160-acre farm, situated around a slough, the old Frio River bed skirting the north-northeast edge of town. Tips had purchased the farm from rancher James Murray, grew cotton, and attempted unsuccessfully to raise hogs. The man with the bucket is a local hired hand. (Courtesy Stanley Stewart.)

36

Charles Tips convinced George Hagn, who owned several gins in Guadalupe County, to build a cotton gin in Three Rivers. At the time, cotton was king, and the fertile black soil in the confluence of the Atascosa, Frio, and Nueces Rivers provided rich yields. Before Hagn's gin was built, cotton had to be freighted to Oakville by ox-drawn wagons. Hagn also served on the townsite's first board of directors. (Courtesy Eugenia Thorn.)

Bales of cotton wait on a railroad platform, ready to be loaded into boxcars bound for factories in the Northeast. Jim Murray sits on the white horse. The person on the right in the buggy may be W.J. Armstrong. It was hard to tell the difference between farmer and rancher in Three Rivers. Before the discovery of oil and gas, folks managed on whatever the land yielded. (Courtesy Stanley Stewart.)

Before the automobile, mules were the main means of conveying loads. Men took pride in their animals and gave them names. Domestic cattle became a staple. In step with the rest of the nation, around the turn of the century, the Polled Hereford, or hornless breed, was valued for its hardiness, beef quality, and dependable reproduction. The gentlemen here are unidentified. (Courtesy Eugenia Thorn.)

When it rained, Live Oak County was a virtual garden of grasses and flowers. Grass grew high and profusely, giving the cattle plenty to eat. Typically, however, long dry spells persisted, which required hauling hay or burning the sharp needles off prickly pear for cattle to eat. Everyone holstered pistols or kept a rifle close at hand to dispatch the ever-present rattlesnake. (Courtesy Eugenia Thorn.)

Like others who moved to Three Rivers, Charles Tips figured he could get rich by raising hogs. The prospects seemed to be a matter of simple arithmetic: the hogs would multiply rapidly, until there were thousands of them for shipping to metropolitan meat markets. According to Tips, however, the plan never seemed to work out, for something typically went wrong when it came time to load the hogs on trains and ship them to market. Not all pig farmers experienced the same disappointment, though. Some of the farmers managed to produce a steady supply of hogs to make the effort profitable. Three Rivers farmers introduced hogs to replace a declining demand for sheep, cattle, horses, and mules. Hogs escaping into the countryside became wild and proliferated. Though many were captured and shipped to meat-packing plants, feral hogs remained an annoyance, but also were used for those hunting for sport and meat. Floyd Weed from the Votaw area is on the ground at left, facing the camera. (Courtesy Eugenia Thorn.)

Charles Tips organized the Live Oak County State Bank in 1914, later renamed the First State Bank of Three Rivers. Congressman John "Jack" Nance Garner (left), former speaker of the house and two-term vice president under Franklin D. Roosevelt (1932 and 1936), purchased shares of stock from Tips for $1,000. During the Depression, as house speaker, Garner interceded on behalf of Tips to save the bank from closing. Tips, only 21 at the time, served as the first bank president until joining the Army in 1917, when he sold his controlling shares to Charles B. Gaddis and Buck West. M.T. "Mack" Buckaloo Sr. subsequently purchased the controlling shares. Mack became the force and guiding spirit of First State Bank. In 1960, Garner gifted his stock to Southwest Texas Joint County Junior College in Uvalde. (Above, courtesy First State Bank; left, Library of Congress.)

Aubrey Lee pitched for the Whitsett baseball team in the 1920s and later moved to Three Rivers. Delivering groceries for the Red and White store, he met Lillian Shipman. The couple, shown at right, married in 1933 and bought the grocery. Young boys riding the running boards of Lillian's car helped deliver advertising flyers. She paid them 50¢, which bought a hamburger, drink, and movie. During World War II, she candled eggs on Saturdays and counted ration stamps on Sundays. Aubrey opened the Three Rivers Locker Plant in 1946. Besides meat, he stored ladies' coats in the summer. Leasing the Gurwitz store, Lillian opened the Three Rivers Dress Shop. Unknown to either when they married, both had ancestors who drew beans in the disastrous Mier expedition during border conflicts with Mexico when Texas was a republic. The Lees were known for their local philanthropy. (Courtesy Margaret Ratliff.)

In 1933, the Boudreau family built and operated the Three Rivers Refinery, which processed crude piped from county oilfields, many drilled by Henderson Coquat. Destroyed by a 1970 hurricane and fire, the plant's remains were acquired and rebuilt by Valero, listed among *Fortune* magazine's 100 best companies to work for. Today, the 400-acre refinery processes crude from the Eagle Ford Shale, replacing foreign oil. (Courtesy Elmo Hartman.)

Whitey (pictured) and Martha Walker lived in tents while he pioneered oil-well cementing with Halliburton during the Kilgore oil boom of the 1930s. Halliburton moved him and his family to Three Rivers in 1943, where he met Henderson Coquat. With Eric Halliburton's blessing, Whitey's Cementers began operation in 1948, cementing casing for drilling rigs in Live Oak and surrounding counties while Halliburton expanded worldwide. (Courtesy Marion Walker.)

In 1922, Three Rivers Glass Company began operation, eventually producing over 75 percent of the beverage and food bottles in Texas. When Charles R. Tips was seeking markets for natural gas and quartzose sand abundant around Three Rivers, he and a group of investors met and contracted Ohio glassmaker H.S. Warrick to build and manage the factory. Mount Rushmore sculptor Gutzon Borglum, who met Tips while living in San Antonio, reportedly designed glass dies for the factory. (Courtesy Elmo Hartman.)

Former employees and citizens congregated in 1973 at the vacant site of the Three Rivers Glass Factory for the unveiling of a Texas State Historical Marker commemorating the first glass factory in the state. Among those at the ceremony are, from left to right, David Jones, Carl Steadman (with pipe), Lee Wiebush, and Lucas Diaz. The company made decorative glass containers for bottling soda, beer, milk, pickled vegetables, and rubbing alcohol. (Courtesy Peggy Hillje.)

This 1922 image is looking south on Harborth Street. J.A. Gurwitz Furniture, seen at left, stood on the east side, across from the public square where the City Municipal Building is today.

After two years in the Russian army, Samuel Lebman emigrated from Russia to escape the Bolshevik Revolution. "Sam" Lebman opened a grocery in St. Louis and, later, brought his wife, Golda, and son, Hyman, to America and opened another grocery. They had two more children, Sarah and Philip. Sam helped his siblings emigrate, and he then did the same for Golda's. Homesick, one Lebman brother returned to Russia. Golda developed respiratory problems, necessitating a move to a warmer climate. Sam, hearing about the glass factory in Three Rivers, moved his family and established a grocery there in 1922. He opened another in Mathis, and when Ball Glass Company bought the plant and closed it in 1937, he opened a store in San Antonio. Philip took ownership of Mathis; Hyman opened a gun and hardware store in San Antonio. The grocery in San Antonio was Sam's last. (Courtesy Phyllis Gurwitz-Davis.)

US Highway 281 eventually came through town on Harborth. (Courtesy Gurwitz family.)

Texas A&M engineering graduate Jack Gurwitz married Sarah Lebman on December 30, 1923. Jack and Sarah moved from Dallas to Three Rivers in 1928 when Sam Lebman offered Jack ownership of his store. Jack converted the business to furniture and dry goods. The family lived in the back of the store, and the downtown area served as the Gurwitz children's playground. To draw customers, Jack placed a Victrola phonograph on the sidewalk in front of the store. Customers kept the Victrola playing all day, especially on weekends. An enthusiastic booster, Jack sat on the Three Rivers school board. Before school buses, Jack used his car to transport players to games. Four of the Gurwitz children, Phyllis, Joyce, Gary, and Bobby, graduated from Three Rivers. The community-minded family sold the Gurwitz building to the city; today, it serves as a community center. (Courtesy Phyllis Gurwitz-Davis.)

Business and family were one and the same for the David Bomar household. His son Royce opened the first service station in Three Rivers and launched three generations of Bomar Texaco consignees. Another son, J.T., graduated from Rice University and joined Royce and their dad. And Ray soon followed in the family footsteps. Ray's all night café and bus stop was begun in conjunction with the service station. Behind the counter in the photograph below, facing the camera, is Ray Bomar (far left). To his left is Mary Roberts followed by the Riley sisters and unidentified waitresses. Ray married Beulah Blackmon, who taught at the Mexican school and helped with the café. Ray added new locations in George West and Oakville. Beulah managed the businesses four years until Ray returned from the 29th Battalion in the South Pacific. Good food and hospitality made Ray's the local meeting place. Couples like Jeannie (Carroll) and Homer Dove began romancing there shortly after Homer's return from the Asiatic-Pacific theater in World War II. (Courtesy Stanley Stewart.)

In 1928, Elmer House ran a confectionery in Three Rivers. He sold the business a year later, clearing $26. After other marginal ventures, Elmer convinced his skeptical father to sell washing machines, an uncommon appliance for his service station. It worked, so additional appliances were introduced, followed by Pontiacs, Buicks, and John Deere tractors. Elmer also ranched and served as county commissioner for Precinct 2 from 1963 to 1970. (Courtesy Charles Yount.)

Next to the Rialto Theater, tall, long-legged Lee Roy Grimes owned a jewelry and watch repair store that was as neat and organized as his groomed, impeccable appearance. His service was fast and precise, giving him time to help his best friend, Tom Kennedy, who owned and directed the local funeral home. Lee Roy helped Kennedy drive ambulance, greet clients, and prepare the deceased for burial. (Courtesy Gloria Grimes.)

Aristéo Ponce, merchant, fled the Mexican revolution with his wife, Juanita, and children for safety in Texas. An advertisement that Charles Tips placed in *La Prensa* for land and opportunities brought Ponce to Three Rivers in 1924. He built several houses, a dance hall, and established a grocery. He returned to Mexico for his mother. Aristéo was known for his kindness and revered for his community service. (Courtesy Maria Ponce-Chapa.)

The Ponce Grocery and Market opened in 1942, offering Mexican and American foods and merchandise. Aristéo's beneficent acts endeared him to the community. Here, the Ponce family poses outside the store. From left to right are (in front, hand on chin) Jesús; (first row) Manuel, Ricardo, Luis, and Aristéo Jr.; (second row) Aristéo Sr., Juanita, Felix, Pietra, Victor, Guadalupe, and Maria. (Courtesy Geneva Ponce.)

Ponce's Baile (dance hall) attracted many on Saturday nights. Outside, in open stalls, locals sold hamburgers, hotdogs, tacos, tamales, and drinks (but no alcoholic beverages). Cinco de Mayo and Dies y Seis de Septiembre extended to all who wished to come. Emma Flores (carrying the American flag) and Maria Ponce (carrying Mexican Flag) began the evening festivities as Conjunto Alegré from Kingsville played "La Marcha de Zacatecas." (Courtesy Geneva Ponce.)

Recognized by Mayor Felipe Martinez and citizens for his community service, Aristéo was honored with a park being named for him. For customers who lacked a means of transportation or suffered from sickness and were thus hindered from coming to his store, Aristéo delivered to them. He also kept lumber to build wooden coffins lined with black fabric and river moss for the deceased when families lacked money. Aristéo never took payment for this service. (Courtesy Geneva Ponce.)

The first Rialto Theater provided entertainment for years without air-conditioning and indoor restrooms. The one-story structure had a light-fringed canopy stretched above the sidewalk. Above the entrance, the projection room was accessed from an outside stairway. After purchasing tickets, patrons entered through double swinging doors, walked up a ramp, and found seats in rows on a floor slanting down from the projection room to the front near the screen. This allowed the stage to be seen over the heads of those in front. Popcorn and drinks were sold just outside the entrance at a stand called Nick's, though everyone called it Mom and Pop's, after the elderly couple who ran it. The first Rialto was replaced in 1948 by a new, air-conditioned Rialto, which included a balcony, an indoor concession stand, and restrooms. (Courtesy Elmo Hartman.)

Opening in May 1948, the new Rialto Theater provided air-conditioning, balcony seating, indoor bathrooms, and the latest projector technology. The first movie was *Scudda Hoo! Scudda Hay!*, in which Hollywood newcomer Marilyn Monroe had her first one-liner appearance. The only operating theater in three counties, the city-owned Rialto shows first-run movies and hosts special events. (Courtesy Mildred Bellows.)

With the true spirit of an entrepreneur, Joe Jones (left) ingeniously managed the Rialto Theater. The array of confections, sandwiches, and goodies awaiting customers made moviegoing doubly enjoyable. Jones created special events for his venue, including beauty pageants, talent shows, and festivals featuring drawings supported by contributions from local merchants. Lucky ticket holders returned often, as did the hopefuls. (Courtesy Elmo Hartman.)

Youthful, enterprising Alfredo and Emilia Guerra (at left above) moved to Three Rivers in 1950, where they raised a family and ran two businesses. Their first enterprise, a Texaco convenience store, provided money to open Sunrise-Sunset Café (below). Affectionately called "Mrs. G" by many residents, Emilia served up a delectable menu of home cooking with a friendly smile. Jocular Alfredo, with his famous smile, presided over what everyone jokingly called the "Idiot's Table," where regulars sat drinking coffee, talking weather, and spinning yarns. The café served the community for 21 years. When Mrs. G retired and closed the café after Alfredo passed away, the chamber of commerce and the mayor of Three Rivers presented her and her family with an official Certificate of Appreciation "for making a difference in the lives of the citizens of Three Rivers." (Courtesy of Emilia Guerra.)

Located in a basin, Three Rivers has experienced 20 floods since 1913. The worst occurred in 1919, 1932, and in 1967 when Hurricane Beulah flooded Three Rivers (above). Both the city and its citizens lost written and photographic history in the Beulah flood. To prevent future flooding, Mayor James L. Nance, serving from 1978 to 1981, directed construction of a flood-control levee, which was completed in 1982 and named in his honor. Because Three Rivers was prone to flooding, in 1949, Corpus Christi proposed building a dam across the Nueces near Sulfur Creek that would have submerged Three Rivers. This was defeated in the Texas legislature in the early 1950s with the help of local representative Jesse F. Gray and oilman Henderson Coquat. Today, Three Rivers remains flood-free. Below, an unidentified woman stands in front of the high school in knee-deep floodwaters caused by tropical storms in the early 1920s. (Courtesy Elmo Hartman.)

Parades drew big crowds, food, and fun. Halloween, Christmas, and the Live Oak County Fair Parade mobilized the whole county to see Sheriff Sam Huff (center) and his deputies lead cowboys and cowgirls, marching bands, floats, and local beauty queens. Merchants, community clubs, and church groups hosted exhibits, skits, food concessions, cakewalks, and many other entertainments. (Courtesy Judge Jim Huff.)

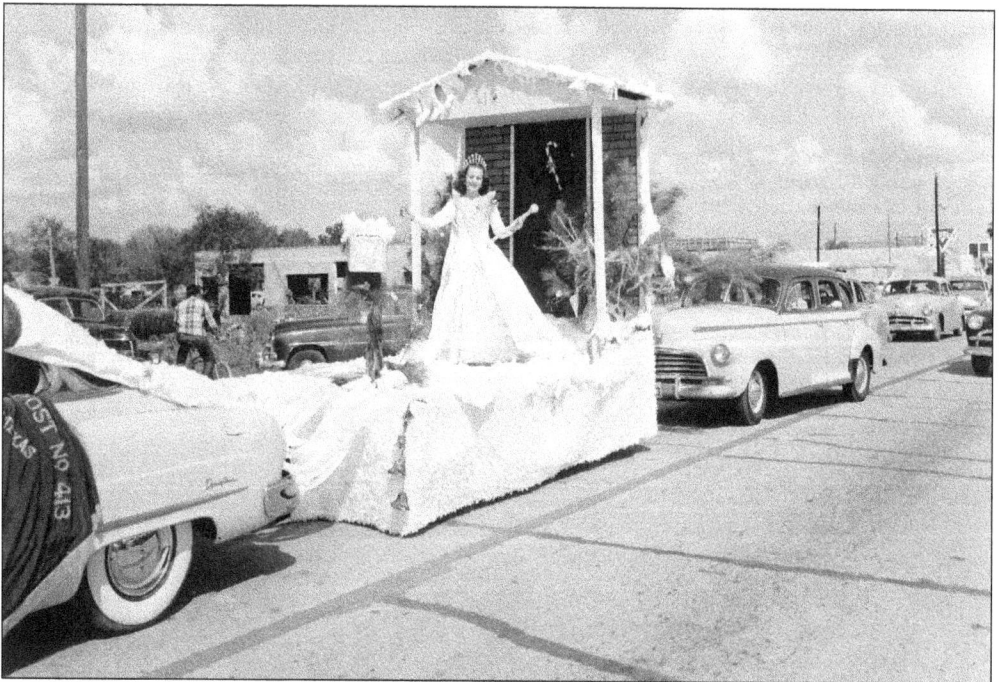

Jo Anne McCalman, sponsored by the American Legion in 1950, appears here as Miss Live Oak County Queen, riding on a Christmas-themed float. Her picture graced the wall of the American Legion hall. Jo Anne was the reigning queen for several years. (Courtesy Elmo Hartman.)

The branch library in Three Rivers started out as a one-room building with few books. Town librarian Vesta Spivey (left) assisted by Vesterlene Ludewig (right), helped Opal Miller, the county librarian, expand the library. The Little Acorn Study Club raised money and sought book donations to fill the shelves. Serving the town and rural areas, the library contributed to children's success in college and in their professional lives. (Courtesy Stanley Stewart.)

Viola Adlof, the first female alderman of Three Rivers, received an official certificate of appreciation from Mayor Erchal Evans for her role as chair of the beautification committee. She galvanized local civic groups and orchestrated efforts that culminated in a first-place Beautify Texas Council Award in 1971. Adlof authored two books and wrote copious newspaper stories about the people of Three Rivers and Live Oak County. (Courtesy Sue Nance.)

Charles Tips built the first Three Rivers schoolhouse in 1913. A one-room structure painted yellow, the school had one teacher, Miss Eva Gallagher (at top above) and 25 students. Initially a seven-year school, it was expanded the next year by unanimous vote to an 11-year school, with six more teachers and its first principal, Professor R.W. Burks. Tips's father, Charles E. Tips, donated 10 acres on the eastern edge of town for a campus. Tips wrote in a brief history how the "public-spirited people" eagerly supported the school. By the end of the first year, five students graduated and the state department of education recognized it for excellence. In the 1920s, Tips's children received "a good foundation, which helped them get college degrees." Below, 11 grades of students for the school year 1929–1930 are assembled before the school. (Courtesy Margaret Cunningham-Custer.)

Originally, separate Hispanic and German community schools taught English as a second language (ESL). Ann Blackmon-Fair (above) and her sister, Beulah Blackmon-Bomar, taught 17 years in the West Ward Mexican School. By 1938, Ann and Beulah developed a progressive language program that began integrating language-proficient students of all grades into the main school. In 1948, only those in first and second grade who exhibited English language deficiencies received separate tutoring. Into the 1950s, Ann Fair taught ESL at the main campus elementary school. She devoted 45 years to teaching in Three Rivers. In 1940, consolidation brought community schools into the Three Rivers Independent School District. Successful consolidation was attributed to progressive-minded school board members, pictured below from left to right: Johnny Schulz, R.E. Stafford, J.A. Gurwitz, L.O. "Tommy" Hartman, E.O. Braune, Otto Franke, H.C. Carraway, and Vestal Odom. (Above, courtesy Stanley Stewart; below, courtesy Elmo Hartman.)

The 1941 Bulldogs played in leather helmets without faceguards and with steel cleats that ripped flesh. Rattlesnakes were sometimes an end-zone hazard. Coached by Weldon Bynum (third row, far left), the Bulldogs played tough teams before loyal fans. One rainy night in 1942 while playing under stadium lights for the first time, the team showed fans their appreciation by pushing cars from a muddy parking lot after a rough home game. (Courtesy Phyllis Gurwitz-Davis.)

The Bulldog Band became an American Top Class A band during Bryce Taylor's 10-year direction. Alumnus Philip Hudson recalls Taylor's leadership as an important factor for many students. In Alice, Taylor built another premier band. At the end of his career, he was recognized by the Texas House of Representatives of the 72nd legislature for his many illustrious championships won at state and national competitions. (Courtesy Margaret Ratliff.)

The Lariat Group performed for halftime shows, in parades, at PTA programs, and on many special occasions. Mothers made matching shirts and blouses. Visible in the back row, Ann Fair (left) and Beulah Bomar, teachers at the West Ward School and later Three Rivers Elementary, sponsored the rope-twirling group. The members dressed as cowboys and cowgirls in Western hats, jeans, and jean skirts. (Courtesy Stanley Stewart.)

After a football or basketball game, these 13 high school students piled on a Willys Jeep. Shown here are, in front, from left to right, Jimmy Casey, James Ritchie, Bill Tope, Otto Huggins (waving), and James Washington (at the wheel). The eight others are unidentified. After-game venues included Ray's Café, the Rialto Theater, Teen Town for dances, and the American Legion north of town. (Courtesy Elmo Hartman.)

Lee Roy Grimes owned a jewelry and watch repair store by the Rialto Theater. When he was not making repairs, he would go to the Mannon Rice Funeral Home to help the owner and director, Tom Kennedy, with funeral and ambulance services. In the office with Kennedy one day, Grimes personally witnessed the conversation that escalated into the highly charged and internationally publicized Longoria Affair. (Courtesy Gloria Grimes.)

In 1924, at age 47, Guadalupe (Lupe) Longoria moved with his wife, Delores, and five children to Three Rivers. Lupe contracted workers for field labor and built houses and barbed wire fences on ranches and farms, providing reliable labor for the community. Later, Lupe, Guadalupe Martinez, and Manuel Muñoz purchased land from Dr. Charles D. Williamson, which they named the Longoria Cemetery. Their heirs continued to manage the cemetery through 2000. (Courtesy Edward Quintanilla.)

A 1949 controversial funeral arrangement between the parents and widow of Felix Longoria, whose remains were repatriated from the Philippines for reburial in Three Rivers, made international headlines. Even though Tom Kennedy, the funeral home director, and Three Rivers were blamed, Three Rivers supported the Guadalupe Longoria family with money and coats for the trip to Arlington National Cemetery where their son, Felix, was interred. It is said this event contributed significantly to the civil rights movement and the 1960 Kennedy-Johnson presidential election. (Courtesy Edward Quintenilla.)

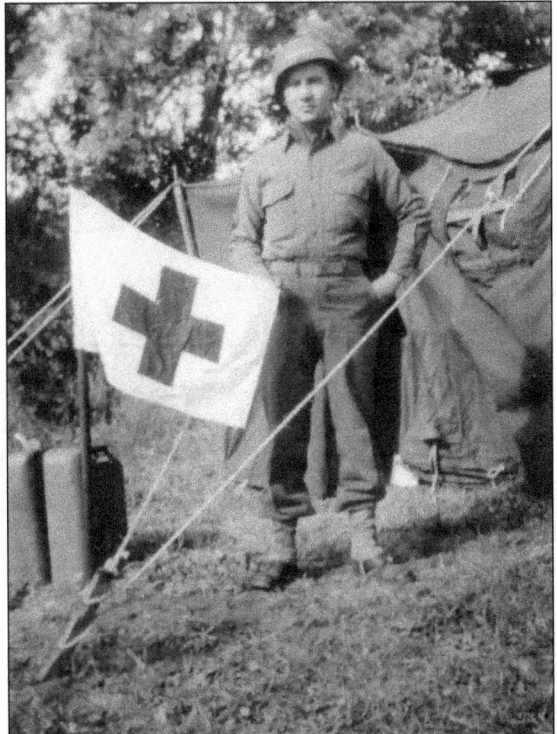

Tom Kennedy, the funeral home owner and director at the time of the Longoria Affair, was a decorated World War II infantry combat medic wounded in the line of duty. He and Three Rivers were exonerated of discrimination by a special legislative commission, the Army Graves Division, and the state Funeral Home Association. Kennedy continued funeral arrangements for approximately seven more years until war injuries and stress disabled him. He died at the age of 43. (Courtesy Jane Kennedy.)

The Little Acorns Study Club provided social and educational outlets for ladies in Three Rivers. Here, Mildred House (left), Thelma Bomar (center), and Lillian Lee share information at one of their meetings. The group sponsored civic projects such as Beautify Texas, for which they won a state award. In addition, they gave a scholarship to a deserving Three Rivers student each year. (Courtesy Sue Nance.)

City aldermen take oaths at city hall. Identified are Jim Nance (center) and Tom Spivey (second from right). When Three Rivers incorporated in 1926, Henderson Coquat was the first mayor, H.T. Harber mayor pro tem, and W.A. Hill secretary. Others involved in the town's incorporation were Dr. Charles D. Williamson, E.G. Majors, and W.C. Matthews. Dr. Williamson served as Three Rivers's first city health officer. (Courtesy Sue Nance.)

After several years of preparation and a yearlong calendar of events, the Crowning Gala of the Three Rivers Golden Anniversary took place on the weekend of July 4, 1963. Shown here are, from left to right, (first row) Prince Timmy Cobb, Princess Mary Reese, King Jesse F. Gray, Queen Pauline Gray, and Court Jester Jimmy Huff; (second row) Mayor James Brice and former mayor James "Jack" Nance. (Courtesy Sue Nance.)

Henderson Coquat, an avid international sports hunter, accepted Tips's call to help build Three Rivers and, in the process, assumed a place among powerful economic and civic leaders in Texas. Besides pioneering and developing the county oil industry, Henderson served as mayor, school superintendent, bank president, and, in 1950, was appointed by Gov. Allen Shivers to the Texas Council on Human Relations. (Author's collection.)

Returning to Three Rivers in 1928 to manage the first glass factory in Texas, Charles Tips purchased a two-story house on Murray Hill. The family hosted friends from business as well as neighbors forced from flooded homes during hurricane season. Tips often spoke of the excellent education his children received in the eight years they lived in Three Rivers. After the glass factory closed and the home burned down, the family moved back to San Antonio. Charles Tips served in World War I and with the Flying Tigers in China during World War II. He was awarded a Bronze Star for his service. Following the war, Tips moved his family to Dallas. He became a successful land developer, erecting thousands of homes and commercial buildings in Houston, Dallas, and San Antonio. (Courtesy Eugenia Thorn.)

Four

GEORGE WEST

VISION OF A TRAIL DRIVER

The Iron Horse made and broke Western towns. With that realization, George West paid $100,000 to the San Antonio, Uvalde, & Gulf Railroad and gave them additional right-of-way through his massive Live Oak County ranch. By late 1913, the train came. West sold 75,000 acres of ranch land and began building the namesake town he envisioned, George West. (Courtesy Patrick Burns.)

Following the Civil War, South Texas was overrun with Longhorns. Cattlemen drove them north to feed a meat-hungry nation. At 16, George West's natural grit and horse sense matured on his first cattle drive. Two years later, the youngest man among his drovers, he contracted with the government to deliver 14,000 Longhorns on the longest cattle drive in Texas history. The first trail boss to drive a herd across the Platte River in Montana, West broke his own trail from there to the Rosebud Indian Reservation. Later, on his Live Oak County ranch, he stocked the best cattle and utilized the latest technology. George and his wife, Kittie Searcy West (above), began with 26,000 cattle in 1880. Based out of his comfortable ranch house (below), West and his cowboys grew the herd to over 80,000 by 1882. (Courtesy Patrick Burns.)

In the above photograph, George West and his niece Clay stop for water at the "Big Tank" supplied by its new windmill. In the flood-drought region of South Texas, watering troughs were critical for all living creatures. The West family was close. Brothers Sol and Ike soon joined George and Kittie, putting down roots in Live Oak County. Life on early ranches meant work for everyone from sunup to sundown. Even though George and Kittie never had children of their own, nieces and nephews were an important part of their lives. Below, on the steps of the Wests' ranch house with their nephews and nieces, George and Kittie West (far left) eat watermelons grown on the ranch. (Courtesy Patrick Burns.)

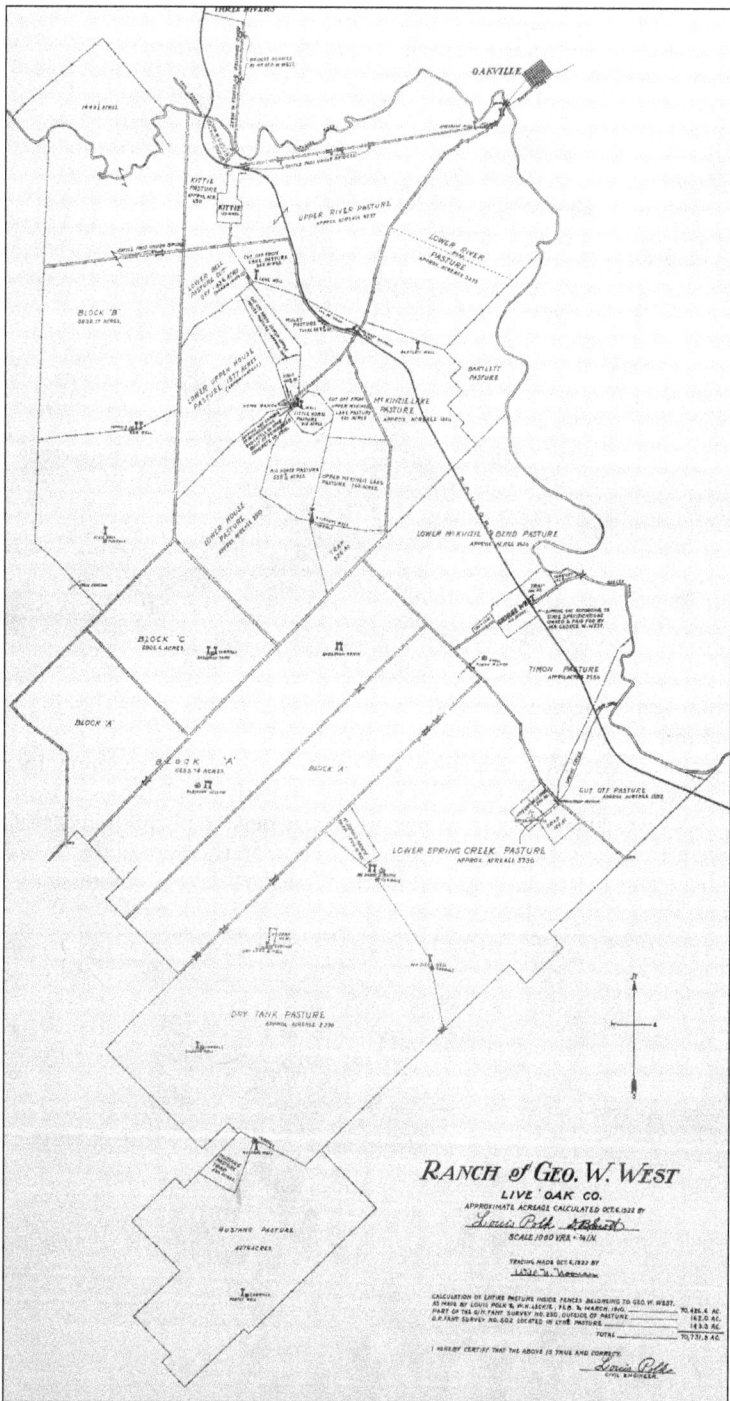

George West purchased about 140,000 acres from Col. D.R. Fant, one of the best-known trail drivers at the time. Ike West, George's youngest brother, later bought 640 acres of Texas state land, which George in turn bought from him. In this way, George increased his holdings until his ranch covered most of Live Oak County and reached into eastern McMullen County. This included the area West later designated for his namesake town. (Courtesy of Patrick Burns.)

George West's family left Tennessee in 1854 when he was three years old. His parents saw Lou, a slave, crying with her baby, Stephen (far left), beside the road. The ordered sale of Stephen would separate them forever. To avoid their separation, George's mother, Mary, insisted on bringing them to Texas. Freed from slavery, Lou (not pictured) and Stephen remained with the West family for the rest of their lives. (Courtesy Patrick Burns.)

Managing the chuck wagon, Stephen (far left) cooked for the cowhands and did other chores around the ranch, including working cattle, mending fences, and wrangling horses. Clay, the young girl standing behind the cowboys in the corner of the pen, watches Stephen and cowhands treat calves against the dreaded tick fever. (Courtesy Patrick Burns.)

Geronimo, George West's prized Longhorn steer, weighed 2,200 pounds. His horns measured nine feet, two inches from tip to tip. Geronimo is representative of the tough, wild Mexican cattle that populated the brush country between the Nueces and the Rio Grande Rivers and that made wealthy the men who were brave and hardy enough to drive the beasts to northern markets. *The Trail Drivers of Texas* credits George West with fattening and marketing more beeves than any rancher in South Texas. Geronimo's breed made it possible for West to build his namesake town. When Geronimo was put down because of a foot injury, West had him mounted for an American bicentennial exhibit. Since then, Geronimo has been exhibited as far away as Russia. Geronimo now stands in a specially built glass case on the George West courthouse lawn. (Courtesy Patrick Burns.)

By 1902, West's success allowed him to build a Victorian mansion in the heart of downtown San Antonio, at the corner of Navarro and Travis Streets. George West grew from cowhand to cattle baron, but times were not always good. During an 1880 drought, the Nueces dried up and West lost 25,000 cattle. Strapping an axe on their saddles, West's cowhands cut the left horn off every dead cow and steer, creating a pile of horns into the thousands before the drought broke. Gulf rains fell, and the West brand surged back, becoming well known throughout the Southwest. George and Kittie lived in the mansion until his death in 1927. Eventually, the house was demolished, making way for San Antonio's commercial growth. (Courtesy Patrick Burns.)

In West's mansion, the grand dining hall was frequently filled with socialites. Debutante dances with stately waltzes and cheerful companions were common. Chandeliers, once gas, were changed to electricity later. Life remained a family affair, with some visits lasting six months or more. The family chuckled at how George and his brothers grew portly once the hardships of their cowman years were behind them. (Courtesy of Patrick Burns.)

San Antonio often chose West honorees for Fiesta's Court of Empires, weeklong festivities honoring Alamo defenders. Princess Kittie West Burns, daughter of Clay, sits ready to throw flowers on the Alamo yard in the 1948 Battle of Flowers Parade. She and other West nephews and nieces attended private schools. In later years, Kittie happily settled in George West with her son, Patrick. (Courtesy of Patrick Burns.)

Roads were vitally important for the new town in the southern part of the county. In this centennial reenactment, the Texas Highway Department demonstrates how mule-drawn graders were used to lay caliche roads connecting George West to Beeville, Goliad, a new town called Three Rivers, on toward San Antonio and other important communities in the county. (Courtesy Patrick Burns.)

The cost of building bridges was not borne by the Texas Highway Department. George West financed two major bridges across the Nueces River and 20 small ones across tributaries and creeks throughout the county. West envisioned his town being the county seat. The roads and bridges connected the county to the town of George West. The vote would come later. (Courtesy Patrick Burns.)

74

The West Hotel ranks high among the achievements of West's new town. Patrons had only to walk from the depot to acquire a room with bath facility, dining room, barbershop, doctor's office, pharmacy, and a bank in the lobby. Fenced in behind the hotel were guest restrooms, plentiful wood for fireplaces, and a pen with poultry for fresh eggs and fried chicken. (Courtesy Patrick Burns.)

Chauncey Zachariah "Chan" Canfield (left) was one of the first businessmen in George West. His family arrived on the first passenger train. Chan built a mercantile store with four rooms in back, partitioned with canvas, for living quarters while his family built a new home. Here, Canfield visits with F.H. Knipling, who owned the Junker Land Company. (Courtesy Robert Canfield.)

Josephine (left) and Emma Canfield's father became the first postmaster, operating the post office in his own store. The sisters are seen above. Emma (right) and her brother Hale ran the store when Chan was no longer able to. The store was a Red and White franchise. Emma, a WAC captain in World War II, later began a smart ladies' shop featuring fashionable apparel that drew women from a tri-county area. Young Josephine took piano lessons in a tent. She later attended San Antonio's Trinity University, graduated from Chicago Musical College, and taught and performed abroad. In George West, she developed talented University Interscholastic League (UIL) competitors, composers, and concert musicians. The young students below are, from left to right, (first row) LeRoy Riser, Tom Kendall, and Maurice Cunningham; (second row) Thomas Miller, Harold Bartlett, Hobart Brewar Jr., and Lloyd Trimble. (Courtesy Robert Canfield.)

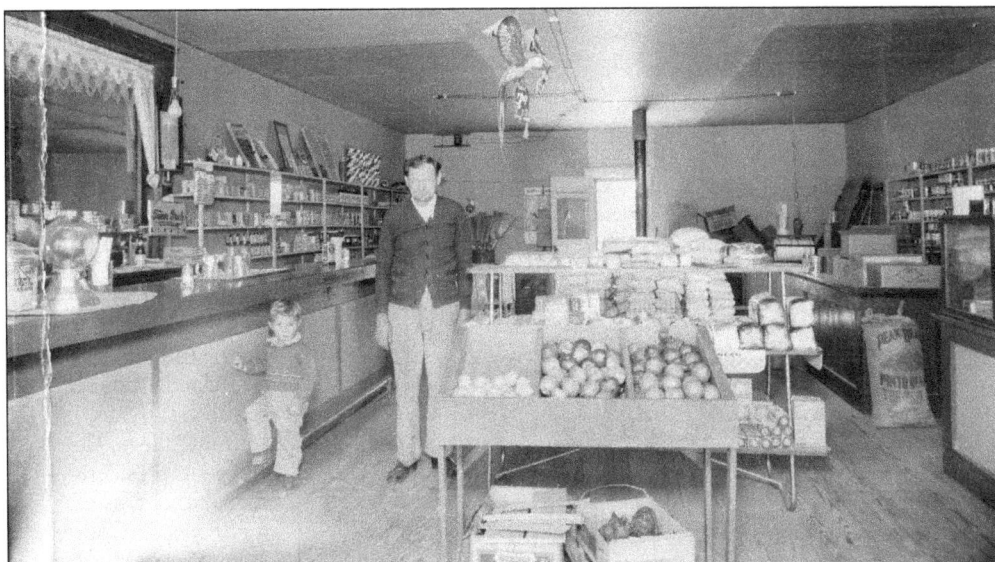

Fred Johnson (left) and Grandpa Woods help in John Johnson's store. Ruth (Woods) and John Johnson, Fred's parents, married shortly before she taught at Mountain View, northeast of Sin Caja Mountain, a mesa west of the county line rumored to have buried treasure. Ruth recorded her experiences in Live Oak County and George West in a delightful book entitled *Memories are Forever*. (Courtesy of Fred and Evelyn Johnson.)

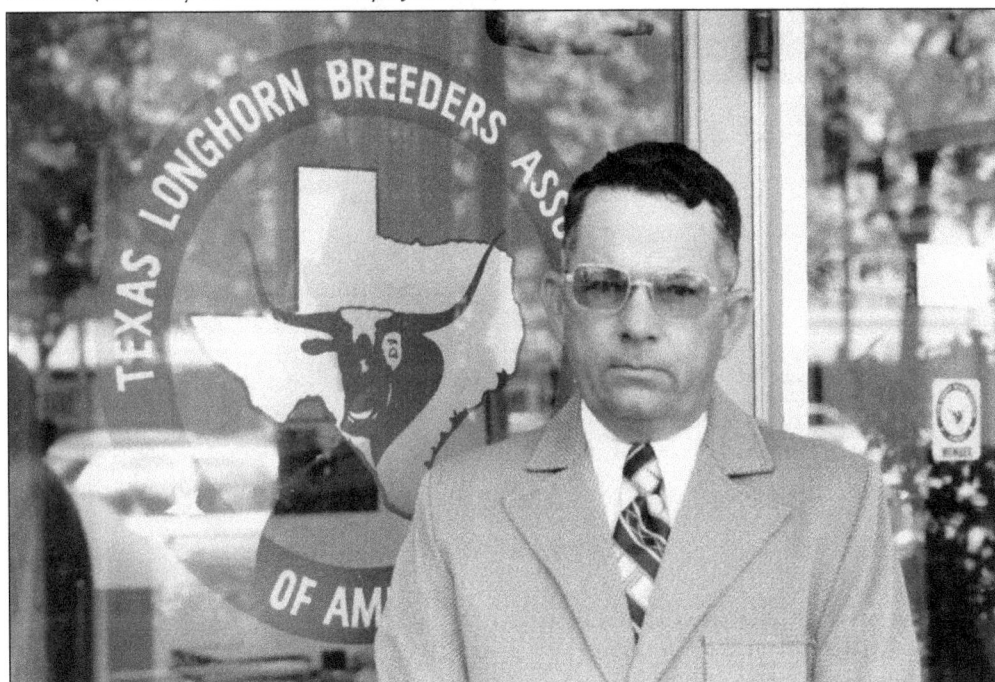

Jim Warren served as president of the Texas Longhorn Breeders Association of America in 1974 and 1975. Breeding Longhorns was a way of life for the Warrens: Jim, Joyce, and sons Wade and T.E. They donated Longhorns to both Sul Ross University in Alpine and Texas A&M University of Kingsville. They participated in George West civic affairs, cattle drives, and other breeder events, and enjoyed working their herd of registered Longhorns. (Courtesy Jim Warren.)

Beginning in 1919, Dr. Hershall LaForge (center) practiced medicine for 21 years in an office next to his home. He became a school trustee, helped develop the Rotary Club, and served as its president. In 1940, LaForge moved his family to Uvalde, where he helped establish Southwest Texas Junior College. He served as president of its board of trustees for 28 years. (Courtesy Armantrout Museum.)

Dr. George Steven Miller sat as Texas house representative for Milam and Roberson Counties in the 28th and 29th legislatures. He brought his wife and his son, John (Ox) Miller, to George West in 1918. For 30 years, "Doc" made house calls, riding horseback when roads were impassable. In Live Oak County, he served as justice of the peace. (Courtesy Opal Miller.)

Walter and Jennie Lamm (below) bought the George West Utilities in 1927 and were joined by her brother, Guy McGee, a year later. The family worked to upgrade the whole town to electricity. Walter engineered, Jennie kept books, and the young ones delivered bills. Mabel Frances, who later married Hale Canfield, even wired a house. After Central Power and Light bought the utilities, the Lamms built an ice plant that serviced the entire county. The high school football team crossed the street for ice shavings after each practice. Sue (Johnson) Holland remembers her fourth-grade teacher taking her to the plant to apply ice to a baseball "pump knot." Walter became mayor of the town. He and Jennie were involved in church and civic organizations. The family actively supported the war effort during World War II. (Courtesy Dorothy Lamm.)

Ernest Lindholm's first service station evolved into the establishment seen in the 1948 photograph above. Lyndon Johnson's freshman senate campaign poster is displayed on the telephone pole. Marley Gillett's trucks nearby are loaded with mesquite posts. Lindholm's stations were real "service stations" where young employees, including the boss himself, greeted customers with a friendly "Howdy!" and rapidly washed windshields, door windows, and mirrors, balanced air in tires, checked water, oil, and brake fluid, and pumped gas at no charge while customers used clean restrooms. Full-time mechanics worked six days a week. Lindholm sold snacks like Lance crackers, bubble gum, cold drinks, and other sundries. His second station was initially owned by former Texas Ranger Leon T. Vivian, then by Marvin Johnson. Vacations sometimes consisted of trips to Junction, Texas, where Lindholm (left) enjoyed the cool waters of the Frio River. (Courtesy Armantrout Museum.)

Will Chaney, who operated the meat market, was proud of his friend's granddaughter, Mary Alyce Owen, who later married Ernest Lindholm's son, Charles. Behind Will and Mary Alyce is the main street of the developing town. In the background at left is the hotel, and just to the right of Chaney, in center background, is the depot. Lindholm's first George West service station, on the far right, has a customer. (Courtesy Armantrout Museum.)

Thomas Nance considered it a privilege to serve on the first George West Independent School Board, created by the Texas state legislature on June 15, 1920. He owned a gas station that offered the first 24-hour service, and the first automobile dealership, the Nance Chevrolet Company. Nance closed the business to serve in World War II. He earned a Purple Heart during the Battle of the Bulge. (Courtesy Sue Nance.)

The Joe Probst family came to George West in the town's first year. The following year, the Probsts entered the mercantile business. Joe built a two-story Neoclassical home for the family. Here, the Probst family members pose for a photograph. They are, from left to right, (standing in front) Josephine "Josie"; (first row) Joe, Helen, and Laura; (second row) Arthur, Alma, and Elwood. (Courtesy Armantrout Museum.)

By 1927, Joe Probst contracted a new two story brick building (left) across from the courthouse for his dry-goods business. The school built by the town's namesake, George West, is visible beyond the building. Arthur Probst later became vice president of the First National Bank. The Probst building was sold to the Pawlik family: James, Edward, and Bobby. They established Pawlik Supply Company, providing an additional lumberyard, well service, and trenching service. (Courtesy John Ed Holland.)

In 1915, the first George West School had one teacher who led 10 students in a small green building. George West erected a new brick school building with classrooms on the first floor and an auditorium upstairs. The classrooms were furnished with the latest technology, including gaslights, slate boards, individual desks with wrought-iron stands secured to the floor, and a full furnace. (Courtesy Patrick Burns.)

George West High School alumnus Thelma (Pugh) Lindholm contributed mightily to the county. Though losing her husband after World War I and her daughter at the age of 10, Thelma taught for 47 years, mentored second-language learners, and is responsible for numerous historical markers and histories, including *The History of the People of Live Oak County, Texas.* She was among the first five female students to enter traditionally all-male Texas A&M College. (Courtesy Peggy Hillje.)

The George West High School class of 1931–1932 poses in front of the school. Among these students are Doris Pugh, May Abbott, Pete Grover, Ruth Walton, Edna Repka, Norine Massey, L'Elladean Davis, Flora Hendrick, Alma Davis, Maurine Lamm, and Ruth Givens. Discipline was tough in those days. Upon returning, expelled students were expected to apologize to the entire student body. (Courtesy Sue Nance.)

Hubert Rankin Reavis directed the first Longhorn band in 1940. Here, the 1949–1950 band sits in front of director W.W. "Odie" Odem. Among those shown are Joyce Lauderbach, clarinet; John Johnson, first trombone; Mattie Lou Clem, second trombone; Evelyn Hines (Johnson), third trombone; Jimmy Jones, saxophone; Lila Bertie, oboe; Myrtle Mae Bartlett, oboe; and Margaret Goynes (Olson), drum major. (Courtesy Evelyn Johnson.)

The 1932 George West Longhorn football team was undefeated. The players are, from left to right: (first row) Buck Nance (right end), Jess Woods (right tackle), David Davis (right guard), Edward Hendricks (center), Davis McKinney (left guard), Jim Nance (left tackle), and Loren Wilder (left end); (second row) Marley Gillett (right halfback), N.B. McKinney (fullback), Oliver Anderson (quarterback), and John Miller (left halfback). Miller became a professional baseball player. (Courtesy Sue Nance.)

The George West High School girls' football team of 1939–1940 poses for a photograph. Shown here are, from left to right, (first row) Bobby Schneider (mascot), Ruth Gaddis (ruled out as kicker for the boys by the UIL), Lois Bush, Delvine Givens (captain), Geraldine Wilson (co-captain), Elsie Muennink, and Marjorie Butler; (second row) Evelyn Edwards, Drusilla Hendrick, Mary Margaret Nance (watergirl), Rena Jane Beal (watergirl), Ruby Virginia Hardwick, Marjorie Wilson, Annie Lee Karger, and Coach Harry Hinton. (Courtesy Armantrout Museum.)

Members of the Future Homemakers of America developed homemaking skills and learned to appreciate the origin of the products they used. In cotton fields, they picked cotton and learned its development, from seed to woven fabric. Here, Joyce Gilstrap (left), Betty Jean Jordan (center), and Margie Stewart show off full-circle skirts made in Inez Bennett's sewing class. (Courtesy Armantrout Museum.)

Future Farmers of America teacher and sponsor Sugars "Tige" Turner Brown (left) inspects Butch Ludwig's show calf. After World War II, Tige graduated from Texas A&I at Kingsville, married Charleen Reagan, and taught high school agriculture for 15 years. Fulfilling 21 years as elementary, then junior high, and high school principal, he finished as superintendent. Tige is remembered as a community builder. (Courtesy Charlie Brown.)

Since almost half of George West students live on farms and ranches, rural life skills and fun are ingrained. They care for and haul animals to the stock barn on traditional Monday livestock auctions, participate in rodeos and fat stock shows, and virtually live in the saddle. In 1972, Jess Elrod won two saddles for roping at the Freer Lions' Club Rodeo. (Courtesy Armantrout Museum.)

The Twentieth Century Club supported civic activities at all levels. Here, Margaret Bednorz presents Stanley New, the president of the high school Key Club, with a check for $25 for the club's work in the City Park. The park was the current project of the Twentieth Century Club, which planned to make it "an attractive and useful recreational unit of the City of George West." (Courtesy Armantrout Museum.)

With all of the activities available in high school, the efforts of the elementary school sometimes go unmentioned. George West Elementary continued Oakville's successful Tom Thumb Wedding fundraiser. Here, fourth grader Alice Ann Allen (Bassett) portrays a bride. The play involved 20 or more students joyfully learning etiquette and tradition. Families throughout the county supported the activity. (Courtesy Alice Ann Bassett.)

Charleen "Charlie" Reagan, Texas A&I (Texas A&M at Kingsville), seen here, was the first female agriculture graduate in Texas. She was undaunted by the gender gap. Following World War II, returning student Tige Brown informed her that she was mistakenly sitting in an agriculture class. She informed Brown that she was right where she belonged. Later, he invited her to T-Jack's, a local A&I hangout. Upon graduation, they married and began teaching in George West. (Courtesy Charlie Brown.)

Opal (Holleman) Miller returned to George West with her husband, John "Ox" Miller, after his major league baseball career. Opal served as county librarian for George West and Three Rivers for the next 42 years. As the library received only meager funding from the county, the Twentieth Century Club added $500 for books, and J. Frank Dobie gifted a number of his books. Opal was selected George West's Woman of the Year in 1980. (Courtesy Opal Miller.)

Members of the Twentieth Century Club wear centennial dresses to Beulah Mae Johnson's house in 1956. Among the ladies are Mary Ann Pawlik, Etaine Harrod, Azalee Bain, Lora Ryan, Betty Wright, Sue Spross, Gertie Iley, Winiola Riser, Anne Hinton, Mable Frances Canfield, Mary Alyce Lindholm, Mary Morgan, Beulah Johnson, and two unidentified. Little girl Sari Ryan is looking at the camera. The two other children are unidentified. (Courtesy Sue Johnson-Holland.)

George West donated property and $75,000 to build the courthouse for his town. In 1919, the people voted to move the county seat from Oakville to George West. In 1920, the courthouse was completed. While the new building was being constructed, the first floor of the West Hotel was leased for county business and the second floor of the schoolhouse for court proceedings. (Courtesy Patrick Burns.)

Historical records were originally kept in large, heavy journals in beautifully handwritten script. Technology took a bold step forward when Effie Ruth (Snider) Lindholm, the first typist in George West, was hired at the courthouse. Today, local records are processed by computers, and many are made available to the world through the Internet. (Courtesy Armantrout Museum.)

Live Oak Title Co. Abstractors insured legal documentation for buyers and sellers during property negotiations in Oakville until the courthouse moved to George West. Otto Roscoe "O.R." Kendall (pictured) then bought the company from Thomas H. Miller and began business in George West. Thomas Miller's son graduated from George West in 1939, joined the Marines, and advanced to the rank of general. (Courtesy Dorothy Lamm.)

Otto's son, Bill, united with his father in the abstract company and continued even after becoming Live Oak County judge. As the county grew, abstracts became more complicated than in the days when property simply changed hands from the state to a single owner. Here, O.R. (left) and Bill peruse the largest abstract they ever issued. (Courtesy Dorothy Lamm.)

Charles Lee Tullis, county sheriff and tax collector (1909–1922), defeated Mexican revolutionaries for the last time in a train shootout five miles south of George West. Tullis regretted the death of Deputy Willie James, killed in the shootout. Tullis's wife, Emma (Lewis), helped with tax collection and with the relocation from Oakville to George West. Tullis later was founding president of the First National Bank of George West. (Courtesy Leslie Walker.)

It was said that "crime did not pay in Live Oak County" when W. Albert Smith served as sheriff and tax assessor-collector (1927–1964). One unorthodox method he employed for keeping the peace was to take teenagers along when making arrests. This practice undoubtedly caused many young men to refrain from illegal mischief. Smith's hallmark was never leaving a case unsolved, even one that took 25 years. (Courtesy Jim Warren.)

"Sam Huff's Hotel," as the county jail was called from 1968 until 1981, offered only necessary amenities. Huff (right) escorts prisoners apprehended for murdering narcotics officer Patrick Allen Randel east of George West. Both prisoners, found guilty, were executed in Huntsville. Sam also served as tax assessor and collector for the duration of his terms. He retired to his first love, ranching. (Courtesy Judge Jim Huff.)

Jim Huff followed the family tradition of law enforcement, becoming Live Oak County judge. Transforming young offenders was the theme of his administration. During Huff's judgeship, the county built an $8 million, 98-bed "restitution center" and made effective use of ankle monitoring. Huff's programs have contributed to a safer county. (Courtesy Judge Jim Huff.)

On the Gillett farm, the young women enjoyed the outdoors and hunting as much as the men in the family. They used shotguns for small game like quail, doves, and rabbits. In this photograph, the women have bagged an owl. Farm and ranch life created gender equality and required that men and women work together if they were to make a living from the soil. (Courtesy Charles Gillett.)

Oil and gas changed life in Live Oak County, and especially in George West, with all the title work the industry generates at the courthouse. The backbone of the profession are the "roughnecks" who run drilling rigs and oilfield equipment. Shown here are, from left to right, Clyde Dartz, Edward Holland, Bunchy Garrison (with his son, name unknown), Doyle Epperson, and Henry Rosebrock. (Courtesy John Ed Holland.)

Faith has been an important part of the county since its inception. When McMullen and McGloin founded their colony, which included Live Oak County, in 1828 under an empresario contract granted by Mexico, it was stipulated that only Catholics could purchase property. So began a tradition Father Matthew Ling continued when he blessed his mother before he left his beloved County Kilkenny, Ireland, for the Texas colony. He ministered to Catholic Europeans and Mexican emigrants alike. However, after independence, Protestants among both groups began settling the colony. (Courtesy Leslie Walker.)

Oil has not been the only boon to the area's economy. Uranium also contributed to George West's boom, because land leases and productive mining made many farmers and ranchers of the county wealthy. Eloy Chapa (seen here in white shirt, rear), the crew foreman of a hole-boring rig, prepares to extract uranium ore from the ground. Chapa worked in the field 17 years. (Courtesy Maria Chapa.)

A lifetime romance began in George West fifth grade. Joyce Gilstrap and Bob Jones graduated valedictorian and salutatorian, respectively, in their class. They went to separate colleges, she to the University of Texas, and he to the University of Corpus Christi, where he was a volunteer fireman. Jones is seen at left. Yet before each began an illustrious career, they came back to George West to be married. The Gilstraps were gifted. Joyce's father, J.C., built homes and the popular Cottage Courts, which became a summer hangout for teenagers around the pool. Jessie Lee, Joyce's mother, drew plans for J.C.'s constructions, including the Methodist parsonage. She also played the church organ. Early on, Joyce's family and Josephine Canfield realized that Joyce was a musical prodigy. Below, Joyce sits in Josephine's studio before her Steinway. (Courtesy Joyce Jones.)

The Wildcats were George West's amateur baseball team. Shown here are, from left to right, (first row) Joe Diaz, Jacob "Jake" Mosqueda, Antonio "Tony" Neros (manager), Manuel DeLeon, and Cosme Diaz; (second row) T.M. Rogstad, Philipi Ybanez, Rogelio "Roy" Chapa, and Rene Chapa; (third row) John Rogstad, Raul "Tripa" Garcia, T.M. Rogstad (coach), Paul Bernal, Bubba LaCour, Cookie LaCour, and K.G. Wendell (coach). (Courtesy Armantrout Museum.)

The Purple Sage, located outside George West, offered sundries, from tincture of iodine to cigarettes and beer. Dances were $1 per person. Popular country western and polka bands played as couples danced across the sawdust-covered floor. John and Ella Trbula (behind the bar) and their daughter, Adeline (front) host guests, from back to front, surveyor Charlie Haberer, J.G. Klebeck, and Bob Riser. (Courtesy Armantrout Museum.)

West Theatre opened on New Year's Eve, 1946. Red River Dave performed with his Western Show Gang; the opening movie was *One More Tomorrow*, starring Dennis Morgan and Jack Carson. Two days later, Alan Ladd starred in *OSS*, a World War II film. The site is currently named the Dobie West Performing Arts Theatre, in honor of Live Oak County author J. Frank Dobie. Plays and other live events are showcased here periodically. (Courtesy Elmo Hartman.)

Riding horseback from farm or ranch to the theater in town on Saturdays was much more fun than riding the bus to school. The Pawlik boys, Everest (left) and Daniel, ride to meet their friends, including Fred Johnson and Buddy Jones. The boys tied their horses to a hitching post near the theater. On one occasion, they discovered that their horses were gone, but the laughing borrowers soon returned them. (Courtesy Mary Ann Pawlik.)

Grace Armantrout (right), park and museum benefactor for the town of George West, moved to town in 1922 to help in the telephone office. She spent another 22 years at the George West Bank, and finally took a position with the highway office. During this time, she acquired eight-and-one-third acres of land and a seven-room house, which she filled with collectibles. The front yard displayed a large cactus garden along Highway 281, while an arbor in the back served as a venue for a band of musicians from the highway department affectionately called her "Highway Boys." She also had a train caboose with many original belongings, completely refurbished by Cosme Diaz. Armantrout donated all of her items to the town of George West. In the below photograph, Grace (second from left) and her brother, Willis (second from right), visit with friends. (Courtesy Peggy Hillje.)

George West's vision came to fruition by subdividing his vast ranch into smaller ranches and farms, and building a supportive town. He sold 15,000–20,000 acres of the West Ranch. Realtors, like the Meyer-Forster Land Company, handled the sales, which West made available on 20-year loans at six percent interest. He introduced modern innovations, such as town utilities, to draw merchants like the Canfields and professionals seeking opportunities. (Courtesy Patrick Burns.)

The West brothers married sisters: Ike (center) married Emma Clay Searcy (left) and George married Kittie Searcy (right). At first, Ike managed the West ranch from Oakville. When the train came to Beeville, moving cattle to market became easier. Bringing the train through George's ranch made it even closer and less costly to deliver cattle to the rail heads. Ike's children, Sol, Albert, Kittie, Buck, and Clay inherited half of the ranch. Their children inherited the other half. (Courtesy West heir Patrick Burns.)

Five

FARMS, RANCHES, AND COWPEOPLE

A TIMELESS ENDEAVOR

Luther Stewart, quintessential cowman, was born in the saddle. He grew up repairing windmills and fences and working cattle on the Cartwright ranch his father managed. Never a rodeo roper, Luther nevertheless easily tossed loops over steers running through brush. The city of Mathis called him to remove rampaging Longhorns from a local park. Skilled and trusted, Luther was the ranchers' choice cowman to "get it done." Horseback and ranching was his life. (Courtesy James and Lonnie Stewart.)

Arriving in New York from Ireland in 1831, Thomas and Margaret Pugh were one of two families completing the Texas journey with John McGloin. Their 1833 farm, near the Nueces River, originally a part of Mexico, is a registered 150-year-old Texas ranch and farm. When their son, William, became the first Live Oak County Civil War veteran to die after the war, his friend, Don Victoriano Chapa, swam the Nueces daily to look after William's wife and children. After Victoriano died, his son continued the pilgrimage. A third-generation Pugh, Charles Madison Pugh, became vicar general of the Archdiocese of San Antonio. In the above photograph, Bill Pugh stands beside the house that replaced the original log home. Below, sixth- and seventh-generation Pugh descendants pose in front of the second house. Shown are, from left to right, (first row) Kathy (Pugh) Howard, Theresa (Henning Pugh) Huebner, and Margaret (Pugh) James; (second row) Bill Pugh and Jim James. (Above, courtesy Peggy Hillje; below, author's collection.)

Edgar James kneels in the field with his nephew, Jimmy, on the registered 100-year-old James Farm. Generational wisdom pays as Jimmy and his brother, Willie, graduated with honors from Texas A&M. Willie earned magna cum laude. The James Ranch and Farm dates from Bridget McGloin's grant and her daughter Agnes's wedding with Will James at Gussetville. The waltz, first introduced in this area at their reception, was received with great derision from their elders. (Courtesy Margaret James.)

Sylvanus Gerard Miller began with 350 acres of an original Mexican grant. He built the first horse ranch in South Texas. His wife, Sue (East) Miller, writes about Terry's Texas Rangers, Miller's Ferry, their Mexican ranch, Pancho Villa, the Civil War, and life near Lagarto in *Sixty Years in the Nueces Valley*. About 18,000 acres of the Miller Ranch is now under Lake Corpus Christi. (Courtesy Gerry Miller.)

Abraham Lincoln was president in 1864 when John Hinnant and Nancy Hudson Miller Hinnant bought a treeless prairie of rolling grass surrounded by caliche peaks. They named the ranch Los Picachos (The Peaks). Before John died in 1877, their son (left photograph), Henry Monroe "Tobe" Hinnant, married Mary Ann Adams, who had arrived from England on June 7, 1876. The couple helped with the ranch. Typhoid fever took Tobe in 1892 when the youngest child, Willie, was only three. With six children and faithful vaqueros, Mary Ann persevered. Below, the six grown children surround their mother in 1907. Shown are, from left to right, (first row) Roy, Mary Ann, and John; (second row) Willie, Rob, Neville, and Bessie. Mary Ann lived to be 108 years old; at 100, she reigned as Queen of the Live Oak County Centennial. (Courtesy Bob and Mary Beth Hinnant.)

Los Picachos Ranch is known for quarter horses. Family members knew horses so well that they were able to identify riders from great distances by the horses they rode. Here, Willie (left), Roy (second from right), and John (right) take a moment's rest from roundup. The person in the supply wagon is unidentified. Mexican nationals living in jacales among the caliche peaks worked with the Hinnants. (Courtesy Bob and Mary Beth Hinnant.)

Behind Bob and Mary Beth Hinnant are the weathered hills, still called Los Picachos. The stamina of Bob's English grandmother, who raised six children and then helped her son, John, with five when his wife died, courses through Bob's veins. Devoted to their heritage and each other, Bob and Mary Beth carry on the ranching tradition started by family patriarch John Hinnant. (Courtesy Bob and Mary Beth Hinnant.)

Sam McWhorter expanded his state land by raising sheep after leaving Fort Merrill. Following Sam's death, his 13-year-old son, Ed, managed the ranch. Ed became a trail driver and escorted Dobie's prize steer, with its nine-and-a-half-foot-wide horns, to the world's fair. McWhorter's registered 100-year-old ranch is managed by great-great-grandson Robert Johnson. Many ranchers found sheep profitable through the early 1900s. (Courtesy Lon Cartwright.)

Little Harry Hinton became a beloved teacher, coach, and principal of George West schools and a county judge for eight years. About 1850, his granddad, Joshua, bought a farm in the bend of Sulphur Creek. Joshua and his father-in-law, John Powell, signed the petition for county status in 1856. Joshua's son, Harry, Little Harry's father, was killed by two jail prisoners one night. Both men were caught and hanged. (Courtesy Byron Hinton.)

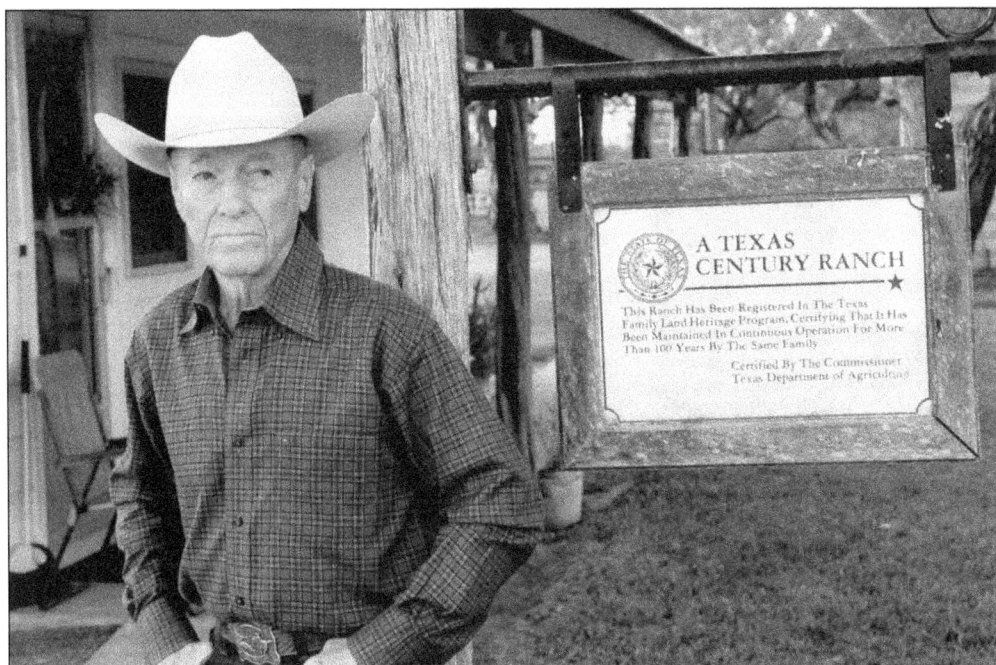

Roy Allen "Buddy" Jones and his spouse, Charon (Buchli) Jones, live on the century-old ranch three miles east of Oakville that his great-great-grandfather bought in 1878. Mississippi-bred ancestors, traveling to California during the 1849 gold rush, stopped on Sulphur Creek, decided to stay, and bought land. When Buddy moved onto the ranch, he paid bills by rodeoing. He still rodeos at 78, with no plans to stop soon. (Author's collection.)

For C.M. and Lena Beall Porter, near Lagarto, century-old farms ran in the family. Love for Live Oak County and ranching, as expressed in "The Roadrunner," won Lena the status of poet laureate for the Texas Federation of Women's Clubs. She also was a distinguished member of the International Society of Poets, their highest honor, and received the Editor's Choice Award from the National Library of Poetry. (Courtesy Jessica Keese.)

John Thomas and Margaret (Nations) Lyne purchased land near George West in 1876. Their children were Thomas John, twins Joseph Eli and William Robert, and Rufus Carrell. In the above photograph, State Agriculture Commissioner Susan Combs presents the Land Heritage Certificate to Leonard Joe "Poochie" and Betty (Upchurch), who live in the original Lyne home. The tribute honors families continuously living on land they have ranched for 100 years or more. At right, members of the Alamo Defenders Descendants Association gather at the Alamo, as they do each March. Leonard Joe Lyne is a descendant of Alamo defender Andrew Kent. Kent and Elizabeth (Zumwalt) had nine children; one was lost during the Runaway Scrape. In the photograph, Leonard stands in front of the Alamo's right corner, wearing a Stetson. His wife, Betty, is to his right wearing sunshades. Betty's family was part of Austin's Old Three Hundred. (Courtesy Betty Lyne.)

William Edward "Bud" and Ophelia (Lewis) Dove began a 100-year farm in Live Oak County about 1905. Grandson Homer Pierre, named also for his Coquat grandfather, made All-Southwest Defensive Linebacker at Texas A&M and received a Bronze Star in World War II. He and his wife, Jeanne (Carroll), purchased Las Palomas, the original farm, from the family. His native collections grew until, now, the home is like a museum. (Courtesy Jeanne Dove.)

Brothers Richard J. and James Madison Dobie established separate ranches in early Live Oak County. Author J. Frank Dobie, son of Richard and Ella (Byler) and the eldest of six children, was born in 1888 and grew up on his dad's ranch. He later managed his Uncle Jim's ranch. Jim Jackson (right), a neighbor rancher, and Jim Warren check out the remains of Richard and Ella's house near Ramireña. (Author's collection.)

Holman Cartwright's (left) dream for Twin Oaks Ranch was to successfully transform huisache, guajilla, and mesquite-infested land into productive grazing pasture for fine cattle breeds. His nephew, Lon (right), continued the work. While the ranch was still under the management of Cyrus Lucas, Holman's wife's father, a massive deposit of oil and gas was discovered that assured the success of the ranch. (Courtesy Lon Cartwright.)

Raising cattle was as much instinct as it was science. James A. "Todd" Stewart (right) proved it time and again as foreman in charge of breeding choice beef cattle. Stewart possessed a practical knowledge on which Holman and Lon depended. The Cartwrights' personal experiment station led to advances in cattle and field production. (Courtesy Lon Cartwright.)

Jimmy Hines, son of Euel and Ila (Walton) Hines, trains his quarter horse, Johnny. Born on "the old home place" of Joe and Ruby (Lemley) Hines southwest of Oakville, as were their last five children, Jimmy now owns Hines Co Feedstore in George West. Several Hines children still live in Live Oak County. Daughter Evelyn and her husband, Fred Johnson, bought Emma Lyne's ranch. (Courtesy Euell and Ila Hines.)

The Pawlik family emigrated from Poland and bought state acreage in West Live Oak County to farm. Everest Pawlik (left), with brother Daniel, graduated from Texas A&M and was the first to introduce liquid fertilizer on a large scale and other advanced farming technologies to the county. Because of the political involvement of him and his wife, Mary Ann, Live Oak became a two-party county in the 1950s. (Courtesy Mary Ann Pawlik.)

Jim Dougherty roped just about anything, winning the National High School Rodeo Calf Roping Championship in 1956.
At Sul Ross College, he won awards in National Intercollegiate Rodeo. Jim roped calves, steers, and team roped in the Professional Cowboys Rodeo Association. In 1914, his uncle James R. Dougherty bought the Reynolds-Foster place in Lagarto, where Jim crossbred Herefords and Brahmas, and developed roping skills. (Courtesy Mary Margaret Campbell.)

Texas Ranger Hall of Fame member Leon Thomas Vivian was proud that he never killed anyone. Vivian became a cowman like his father, then a Texas Ranger. He and Nellie (Morris) had three sons. Nellie managed the ranch while Leon patrolled the Rio Grande during World War II. Two sons became colonels; one, flying B-24 bombers, was captured, but escaped. A third son became president of Gulf Oil. (Courtesy Jim Warren.)

Six

LIVE OAK FOLKS
LEAVING GLOBAL FOOTPRINTS

The passionate folklore of the West in the work of J. Frank Dobie, "Mr. Texas," emanates from his birth on the Live Oak County ranch where he grew to manhood. A Medal of Freedom recipient for 26 works written at the University of Texas, Cambridge in England, and schools in Oklahoma, Germany, and Austria, Dobie is credited with saving Longhorns from extinction and for UT's burnt orange and white school colors. (Courtesy Michener Center for Writing.)

John Miller, 1933 George West graduate, earned the nickname "Ox" for winning both games of a professional doubleheader. He pitched (1937–1954) for the St. Louis Browns, Washington Senators, and Chicago Cubs. After a pitching injury, Ox played and coached locally. His Babe Ruth teams won state championships, qualifying six times for the World Series. The George West High School baseball facility is named John "Ox" Miller Field. (Courtesy Opal Miller.)

Carroll and Cora (Kitchen) Jones, early Texas Baptist pioneers, met and married at Baylor, and then began working a small Live Oak farm while Carroll pastored five churches, preaching alternate Sundays. He was a founding trustee of the University of Corpus Christi in 1947. Cora wrote *What God Hath Wrought: A History of Blanco Association 1873–1973*. The Jones family heirlooms are displayed at Baylor University. (Courtesy Bob and Joyce Jones.)

Jessy Franklin Gray Sr. taught at the age of 16, and after World War I officer's training, married Pauline Campbell, his former Oakville student. Gray became superintendent of Three Rivers ISD and vice president of First State Bank. A three-term state legislator, he prevented Corpus Christi from submerging Three Rivers in a reservoir and requested a legislative investigation into alleged racial discrimination. The issue, broadcast nationally, exonerated a funeral home director and Three Rivers. (Author's collection.)

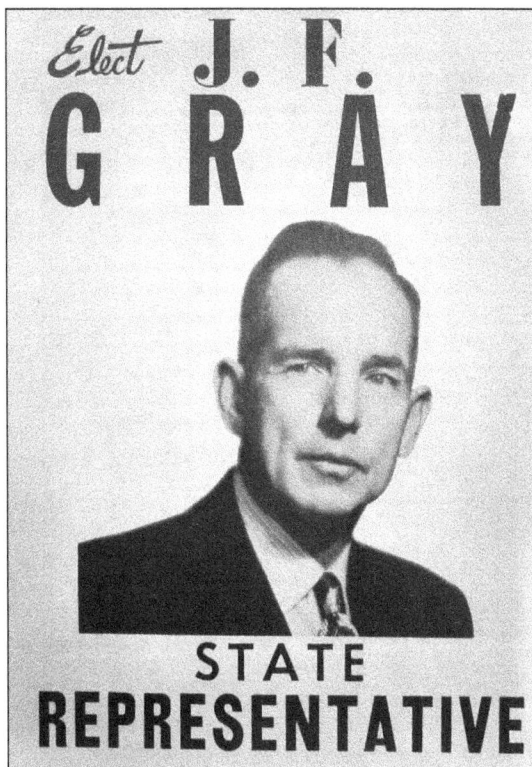

Elect **J. F. GRAY**

STATE REPRESENTATIVE

J.F. Gray, immortalized in poem by his men, received the Purple Heart and Silver Star for saving the 360th Infantry of the 90th Division. He received one of France's highest World War I honors for the liberation of Saint Mihiel. When notified, he wrote Saint Mihiel's mayor to add the infantry to the monument erected by the town. Because of World War I injuries, he served stateside during World War II. (Courtesy Eddie Davis, PhD.)

Patty (Forehand) Reagan, lifetime member of the American Cancer Society, became the first woman Texas chair and was elected to the national board of directors. She worked throughout the country with dignitaries like Tom Landry, the Dallas Cowboys' legendary coach. In 1985, she received the highest National Volunteer Leadership award for the society. Reagan continues volunteer efforts through the Live Oak–McMullen Relay for Life. (Courtesy Patty Reagan.)

At age 14, Kurt House began collecting Old West relics. He later turned the hobby into a business of buying, selling, trading, and appraising antique guns and other Western trappings. He has written hundreds of articles, six books, a screenplay, and produced three documentaries about frontier life on the Nueces Strip. He recently replicated an 18th century–style Spanish mission he plans to make into a living history center for children. (Courtesy Kurt House.)

Charleen "Charlie" (Reagan) Brown's great grandfather, Dr. Green Pryor Reagan, built a Reagan heritage, which was written about by Rocky Reagan in *G.P. Reagan, Country Doctor*; *Rocky's Chuck Wagon Stories*; and *Rocky's Yarns*. Texas A&I seniors expected a trick-roping performance from freshman Charlie. Terrified, she almost quit school until her father, Pryor, taught her. Charlie's trick and flame-roping performances lassoed a Cowgirl Hall of Fame nomination. (Courtesy Charlie Brown.)

Texas A&M recognized Three Rivers High graduate Lee Walker for his thirst of knowledge and, at six feet, nine inches, his dominance in basketball. *The Sporting News* ran this photograph, not because it displayed Walker's prowess, but for his reading Russian and for majoring in nuclear physics. Walker's passion for learning began with dusty encyclopedias and the "wonderful teachers in Three Rivers" who stimulated his intellectual vigor. Graduating from Texas A&M with a degree in physics in 1963, he received funding for postgraduate work in nuclear physics. His MBA came from Harvard. Walker realized his initial successes early as an entrepreneur, then became the first president of Dell Corporation, and later an award-winning lecturer at UT Austin in entrepreneurship and civic engagement. Special projects with the City of Austin led to his being named "Austinite of the Year" by the chamber of commerce. Walker received a lifetime achievement award from the Texas Nature Conservancy for decades of environmental leadership. (Courtesy Lee Walker.)

Col. Patrick "Pat" Nance, like his dad, graduated from Texas A&M. He entered the Air Force flying fixed-wing jets, then helicopters in special operations behind the lines in Vietnam. His career included wing commander in the Philippines, an air planner in the operation that freed Panama from Noriega's dictatorship, the Iranian rescue mission, and Patrick Air Force Base commander during the space shuttle program. Retired, Nance serves where volunteers are needed. (Courtesy Sue Nance.)

Betty (Reynolds) Dickinson's musical gift was refined with training by her aunt Gladys Cunningham and Miss Josephine Canfield. Dickinson became a concert duo-pianist, performing widely, and taught piano for 33 years. She generously played for multiple public occasions. Dickinson is founding member and past president of Coastal Plans Music Teachers' Association and cofounder and past president of Celebration of Art and Music of Live Oak County. (Courtesy Betty Dickinson.)

Coach Mack T. Roberson's family moved to Three Rivers in 1914 with the railroad. His father and Uncle Felix managed a lumberyard and cabinet shop. Graduating in 1943, Mack attended Sul Ross College before coaching Falfurrias High School football. His many achievements included three consecutive district football titles. In 2006, he was inducted into the Costal Bend Coaches' Association Hall of Fame. (Courtesy Mack T. Roberson.)

Daylon Hicks from Three Rivers became "America's Youngest Singing Cowboy" when popular western singing star Red River Dave heard him play guitar and sing at age 12. Songs like "You Broke My Heart" and "Faded Roses" landed Daylon a television appearance and two radio programs of his own. After serving in the Army, he and his wife, Lynda (Wilson), became missionaries to Haiti and South America. (Courtesy Daylon Hicks.)

Joyce (Gilstrap) Jones, internationally acclaimed concert organist and composer, performed in 47 states and 12 foreign countries. The venues she played in included the Dallas Symphony Orchestra, Mormon Tabernacle Choir, Crystal Cathedral, Notre Dame Cathedral, Chartres Cathedral, and the San Francisco Symphony Orchestra. Jones began piano with her mother and Josephine Canfield. She wrote compositions at an early age, playing one at elementary graduation in George West. She broke her hand and began playing organ. She has written 19 books of organ music and instruction. She is organist in residence and Joyce Oliver Bowden Professor of Music at Baylor University. Joyce says her career and her husband's, Army Chaplain Robert Jones, meshed beautifully, whether in the States or abroad, even when it meant "red-eye" flights. She received the Award of Merit, the highest award given by Mu Phi Epsilon, the international professional music fraternity. (Courtesy Joyce Jones.)

Harry Geffert, nominated for 2013's Texas State Visual 3-D Artist, calls his exhibit at Pillsbury and Peters Fine Art Gallery "The Fiery Art of Harry Geffert: The Three Rivers Series." Geffert's highly recognized bronze work shows the influence of his Simmons farm life near Three Rivers. Geffert liked to carve intricate caricatures from wood and won state whittling competitions in high school. He studied art at Southwest Texas State and New Mexico Highlands University, and taught sculpting at Texas Christian University for 27 years. His art is widely collected in public and private galleries, including the Dallas Art Museum, Museum of Fine Arts–Houston, Modern Art Museum of Fort Worth, and private collections of the Richard Barretts and the Bryant Handleys. His Texas Sculpture Garden is at the Moody Gallery. Geffert operates from his own Green Mountain Foundry in Crowley, Texas. (Author's collection.)

Robert "Bobby" Gurwitz loved sports. An all-state player in high school basketball and football, Gurwitz was drafted by the University of Texas–Austin. Sportswriters described the 155-pound Gurwitz as "one of the most spirited football players in Longhorn history." As president and co-owner of prestigious clothier Julian Gold, Gurwitz has directed the company's four stores for 50 years in the same spirited way that he played on the field. He does not plan to retire. (Author's collection.)

John Spivey wanted to travel and see the world that he read about in *National Geographic*. A Three Rivers high school valedictorian, he obtained an aerospace engineering degree. Ramjets and reaction control rockets comprised his first work. As senior design engineer on Navy A-7 and S-3 carrier aircraft, he did indeed travel. With his engineering days behind him, Spivey, with his spouse, Anna (Townsend), travels worldwide, visiting the places he once read about. (Courtesy John Spivey.)

James Warren, local and regional archaeologist, brings the Southwest past to life by locating and restoring places of historical importance. Here, he stands beside a restored pioneer home on the Temple Ranch in Duval County. The highway department sought Warren's expertise during a study of ancient Indian artifacts excavated from Loma Sandia. He unearthed a mastodon tusk on Kittie West Burns's ranch. It is displayed in the George West Armantrout Museum. (Author's collection.)

John Sisk, a longtime Live Oak resident, thought his life was over when he fell from a high-rise scaffold and broke nearly every bone in his body. While recovering, he decided to attend auctioneer school to fulfill a lifelong interest. He organized Sisk Ministries to share his faith through song and testimony. In 2012, Sisk was elected to the Texas Auctioneer Hall of Fame. (Courtesy John Sisk.)

World champion cowboy Phil Lyne, a 2004 Texas Rodeo Hall of Fame inductee, is the only cowboy to win the National Finals Rodeo titles in three categories: bull-riding, calf-roping, and steer-roping. He astonished competitors by winning roping competitions from horses borrowed on arrival. Lyne's record fastest calf-rope and tie-down, in 1971, was 8.5 seconds. His amount of prize money for that one year was $60,000. Phil costarred with Larry Mahan in *The All American Cowboy*, a Disney documentary featuring rodeo rivalry. On the 7L (Lyne) Ranch that his great-grandfather began in 1876 just outside George West, Phil learned to ride and rope. By the age of 12, he competed and won at least 45 trophies within the next 12 years before becoming the world's best. He retired at about 27 and taught aspiring cowboys and made special appearances. He lives on his own ranch in Cotulla. (Courtesy Betty Lyne.)

Nolan Ryan, legendary pitcher, chose famous Ray Ranch in Live Oak and McMullen Counties to fulfill his ranching aspirations. He knew about Ray Ranch from his collection of J. Frank Dobie's books. Ryan added Nolan Ryan's Waterfront Restaurant, overlooking Choke Canyon Reservoir, where he served branded Beefmaster steaks until he became an owner and executive manager of baseball's Texas Rangers. A surprised Ryan received the Chester A. Reynolds Award from the National Cowboy Museum in Oklahoma City, awarded "to a living person who has perpetuated the ideals, history, and heritage of the American West." In spite of Baseball Hall of Fame honors for many unbroken records (fastest baseball, clocked at 100.9 miles per hour; 5,714 strikeouts; seven no-hitters; 12 one-hitters; and the only player with a retired uniform from three teams), Ryan remains focused and humble. (Courtesy Nolan Ryan.)

BIBLIOGRAPHY

Adlof, Viola. *Lisa's Texas Grandma*. Boerne, TX: The Highland Press, 1963.

Chipman, Donald E. *Alvar Nuñez Cabeza de Vaca*. Denton: Texas State Historical Association, 2012.

Dobie, J. Frank. *Cow People*. Boston: Little Brown and Company, 1964.

House, Kurt. *Various Papers on Live Oak County*. San Antonio: Self published, 1970–1980.

Hunter, J. Marvin. *The Trail Drivers of Texas*. Austin: University of Texas Press, 1925.

Johnson, Ruth. *Memories are Forever*. Toronto: Monument Press, 1987.

Lindholm, Thelma. *Live Oak County Centennial*. George West: Armantrout Museum, 1956.

Lindholm, Thelma and Viola Adlof, ed. *The History of the People of Live Oak County, Texas*. Publisher unknown, 1982.

Miller, S.G. *Sixty Years in the Nueces Valley*. San Antonio: Naylor Printing Company, 1930.

New, Hattie Mae. *Lagarto: A Collection of Remembrance*. Corpus Christi, TX: Quantam Kopies.

Olson, Margaret. *Texas Roots*. Easley, SC: Southern Historical Press, 1999.

Robinson, David. *A Little Corner of Texas*. Tulsa, OK: John Hardin Publishers, 1991.

Sparkman, Ervin. *People's History of Live Oak County, Texas*. Mesquite, TX: Ide House, 1981.

Taylor, Anna, and Highley, Cheryl. *Archeological Investigations at the Loma Sandia Site* (41LK28). Austin: The University of Texas at Austin, 1995.

The Handbook of Texas Online, The Texas State Historical Association, University of North Texas, Denton, Texas, www.tshaonline.org.

Visit us at
arcadiapublishing.com